PRAISE FOR *YOUR LONGING*

"This book is a gift for our souls."

—BOB GOFF, *NEW YORK TIMES* BESTSELLING AUTHOR OF
LOVE DOES, EVERYBODY ALWAYS, AND *DREAM BIG*

"*Your Longing Has a Name* shows us a unique way to shift our perspective when looking at our purpose and calling, bringing hope and light into whatever situation we may be in. Dominic gives us a reminder of who God says we are."

—LEVI LUSKO, LEAD PASTOR AT FRESH LIFE CHURCH AND BESTSELLING AUTHOR
OF *THROUGH THE EYES OF A LION* AND *THE LAST SUPPER ON THE MOON*

"Dominic Done is a thinker for our time. His ability to apply the Christian vision to our deepest, darkest secrets is a beautiful gift to the church. Plus, he can *write*. Open your heart to this book."

—JOHN MARK COMER, *NEW YORK TIMES* BESTSELLING AUTHOR
OF *LIVE NO LIES* AND FOUNDER OF PRACTICING THE WAY

"Page after page of *Your Longing Has a Name* is filled with poetically crafted wisdom that will saturate your beaten and bruised soul with what can only be called beauty—the kind of beauty your soul was made to crave."

—DIANE COMER, COFOUNDER OF INTENTIONAL PARENTS INTERNATIONAL

"*Your Longing Has a Name* is not only insightful and encouraging but also beautifully written. It offers seven practical ideas, rooted in Scripture, to help you experience a truly flourishing life as part of God's story."

—SEAN MCDOWELL, PHD, APOLOGETICS PROFESSOR AT BIOLA UNIVERSITY
AND AUTHOR OF OVER EIGHTEEN BOOKS, INCLUDING *CHASING LOVE*

"Dominic Done addresses the heartache and confusion in today's culture and the health of what matters most—our soul. He brilliantly unveils a timely yet ancient truth, reminding us that there is a road to redemption, a journey to joy, a person to follow—and that our longing has a name."

—JEREMY ROLOFF, *NEW YORK TIMES* BESTSELLING AUTHOR OF *A
LOVE LETTER LIFE* AND COFOUNDER OF BEATING50PERCENT

"Dominic Done weaves together spiritual truths and fascinating research with his own crystalline way of turning a phrase, and the result is a singularly hope-filled creation. The way he illuminates the connection between genuine soul care and the flourishing life is incredibly profound and wise."

—KRISTEN STRONG, BESTSELLING AUTHOR OF *GIRL MEETS CHANGE*, *BACK ROADS TO BELONGING*, AND *WHEN CHANGE FINDS YOU*

"*Your Longing Has a Name* is relevant, practical, and helpful for everyone who has ever gone through a difficult season of life. Which is every single one of us, so I highly, highly recommend this book for everyone."

—SHANE PRUITT, NATIONAL NEXT GEN DIRECTOR FOR NORTH AMERICAN MISSION BOARD AND AUTHOR OF *9 COMMON LIES CHRISTIANS BELIEVE*

"We live in times when our souls are languishing, and not through lack of effort. More is spent on self-improvement than ever before, yet we see the signs of decay everywhere. What shape is your soul these days? My friend Dominic Done has done us all a great favor in writing this look at life through the lens of one of Jesus' best friends: Peter. Who better than Peter to guide us into the life and ways of Jesus? We are designed by God himself to walk with him as beloved children."

—KEVIN PALAU, PRESIDENT AND CEO OF LUIS PALAU ASSOCIATION

"Dominic Done is the perfect person to write *Your Longing Has a Name* because of his keen ability to make important connections between the Scriptures and our unique experiences. This beautiful book invites the life of God into your soul."

—DANIEL FUSCO, PASTOR, TV AND RADIO HOST, AND AUTHOR OF *CRAZY HAPPY*

"*Your Longing Has a Name* is a delightful read that will no doubt help many people connect more deeply with God! Dominic Done's smooth writing style and vivid illustrations demystify the process of growing in spiritual maturity."

—CARMEN JOY IMES, ASSOCIATE PROFESSOR OF OLD TESTAMENT AT BIOLA UNIVERSITY AND AUTHOR OF *BEARING GOD'S NAME*

"*Your Longing Has a Name* is a beautifully written invitation to rest fully in our Father, who has given us everything we need. This book is a must read for every languishing heart. Every sojourner searching for peace in this chaotic world. Every desert dweller who longs for rain to fall and flourish the seeds already planted in their soul."

—MELANIE DOBSON, AWARD-WINNING AUTHOR OF
CATCHING THE WIND AND *THE WINTER ROSE*

"My soul needed this book! If you're feeling exhausted or overwhelmed, Dominic is a trustworthy guide whose words are true, his prose beautiful, and his vision captivating of the God for whom your heart aches."

—JOSHUA RYAN BUTLER, AUTHOR OF *THE SKELETONS IN GOD'S CLOSET*
AND *THE PURSUING GOD* AND LEAD PASTOR AT REDEMPTION TEMPE

"We live in a world constantly and incredibly bombarded every day by powerful identity-shaping messages that influence us, whether we realize it or not. I am so thankful that Dominic Done has written a biblically based guide to understanding our place in God's story and how God created us to live, all while the culture pressures us to be someone else."

—DAN KIMBALL, AUTHOR OF *HOW (NOT) TO READ THE BIBLE* AND
SEVERAL BOOKS ON LEADERSHIP, CHURCH, AND CULTURE

"We are living through times that test the soul. Full of wisdom and insight forged in the furnace of his own experience, Dominic Done's book will provide anyone struggling to make sense of their journey with a road map to forming a resilient, integrated, and flourishing life."

—JUSTIN BRIERLEY, BROADCASTER, SPEAKER, AND AUTHOR OF *UNBELIEVABLE?:
WHY, AFTER TEN YEARS OF TALKING WITH ATHEISTS, I'M STILL A CHRISTIAN*

"*Your Longing Has a Name* is filled with hope, and people need hope—especially today. Through Scripture, history, and personal stories, Dominic Done beautifully and compellingly points us to the source of all hope, Jesus. I loved this book, and I know you will too."

—BRIAN BRODERSEN, PASTOR AT CALVARY CHAPEL COSTA MESA

"Grounded in the timeless wisdom of Scripture, *Your Longing Has a Name* is a must read for anyone seeking clarity on God's will, purpose, and calling for their life. With humor, poetic reflection, and pastoral care, Dominic uniquely draws us into the story of God and makes profound truths accessible."

—JOSE ZAYAS, PASTOR OF TEACHING & LEADERSHIP AT 26 WEST CHURCH

"Into our age of deep exhaustion, and into a society that has lost its soul, Dominic Done speaks. This book is sensitive, intuitive, and transformative. A word of life for all those who will have ears to hear."

—DANIEL GROTHE, AUTHOR OF *THE POWER OF PLACE* AND ASSOCIATE SENIOR PASTOR AT NEW LIFE CHURCH

"Dominic Done continues his work of pursuing faith by exploring how the deep longings of our empty, tired soul can be filled—now and for always. It's Moses' ancient cry, 'Show me your glory,' meeting the seven gifts of 2 Peter 1 that bring forth the deep flourishing of our soul."

—GERRY BRESHEARS, PHD, PROFESSOR OF THEOLOGY AT WESTERN SEMINARY

"With lyrical prose and powerful insights, Dominic Done points to a road map for the soul in an often-overlooked passage of Scripture. I finished *Your Longing Has a Name* filled with confidence that a life of meaning and fulfillment, while not easy, is possible. God used this book to breathe fresh life into my soul. I know it will do the same for many others too."

—DREW DYCK, AUTHOR OF *YOUR FUTURE SELF WILL THANK YOU* AND EDITOR

"Deep in our hearts is an ache—for meaning, for purpose, for love itself. With the tenderness of a pastor and the precision of a theologian, Dominic Done helps us recognize how God speaks to us in our longings and forms us in his love. This is a book that has the power not only to inform your mind but to awaken your heart."

—DR. GLENN PACKIAM, ASSOCIATE SENIOR PASTOR AT NEW LIFE CHURCH AND BESTSELLING AUTHOR OF *THE RESILIENT PASTOR* AND *BLESSED BROKEN GIVEN*

"Few would dare say that the world is going the way it is *supposed* to go. Indeed, things are broken. But the Christian narrative poignantly described in *Your Longing Has a Name* refuses to accept the status quo. We worship the God who longs for us—and whom we were made to long for."

—A. J. SWOBODA, PHD, ASSISTANT PROFESSOR OF BIBLE, THEOLOGY, AND WORLD CHRISTIANITY AT BUSHNELL UNIVERSITY AND BESTSELLING AUTHOR OF *AFTER DOUBT*

"*Your Longing Has a Name* invites us on a journey to find our purpose in this ever-changing world. Using the Bible as his guide, Dominic graciously and masterfully reveals through story how the character, nature, and beauty of Jesus serve as the true longing of our soul."

—KYLE DIROBERTS, PHD, AUTHOR OF *THE SECRET TO PRAYER* AND PROFESSOR OF THEOLOGY AT ARIZONA CHRISTIAN UNIVERSITY

"We live in a culture obsessed with flourishing, yet it's hard to say what it really is and why it seems just out of reach. With keen biblical insight and practical know-how, Dominic Done develops a much richer, expansive view of flourishing, showing how our deep hunger for God is actually the center of our quest for happiness."

—JOSEPH CLAIR, PHD, EXECUTIVE DEAN OF THE CULTURAL ENTERPRISE AND ASSOCIATE PROFESSOR OF THEOLOGY AND CULTURE AT GEORGE FOX UNIVERSITY

"In a culture permeated with personal improvement strategies comes a biblically saturated, joyous path to being a Jesus disciple. Dominic Done engages us with his witty humor, education, and wonderfully weird experiences to entice us into a very attainable journey to live a flourishing life."

—MATT HEVERLY, LEAD PASTOR AT EDGEWATER CHRISTIAN FELLOWSHIP

"Through his own story of heartbreak and breakthrough, Dominic Done reminds us—going all the way back to Jesus' first followers and closest friends—that God has something beautiful waiting for us on the other side of not giving up."

—DAVID GRECO, COMPASSION INTERNATIONAL CHURCH PARTNERSHIP MANAGER

"Dominic Done unpacks what it means for each of us to live into the story for which we were created. Rooted in God's wondrous love for each of us, the way of flourishing becomes clear. In saying yes to what God intends for us, life takes on right courses and new vistas."

—PAUL N. ANDERSON, PROFESSOR OF BIBLICAL AND QUAKER STUDIES AT GEORGE FOX UNIVERSITY

"Many of us, including leaders and families, have been deeply wounded by performance alone and less care for the soul. Dominic calls us out of the darkness to see the internal dynamics of the soul's health as the springboard of life and true success."

—DR. CHARLES B. MUGISHA, FOUNDER AND PRESIDENT OF AFRICA NEW LIFE MINISTRIES

"Jesus promised us abundant life, but if we are honest, most of us don't often experience that abundant life. Dominic Done provides a practical path forward on how to flourish the way that God intends."

—ERIC CARTIER, SENIOR PASTOR AT ROCKY MOUNTAIN CALVARY

"*Your Longing Has a Name* is a compelling reminder of the story we were made for, the one that captures our hearts, souls, and lives with a beautiful truth. Dominic Done encourages us to dare to hope in a world tinged with the grey of uncertainty, expectant that we will find more than we longed for."

—SARAH YARDLEY, MISSIONS AND MINISTRY LEAD AT CREATION FEST UK AND AUTHOR OF *MORE CHANGE*

YOUR LONGING HAS A NAME

YOUR LONGING HAS A NAME

Come Alive to the Story You Were Made For

DOMINIC DONE

W PUBLISHING GROUP

AN IMPRINT OF THOMAS NELSON

Published in Nashville, Tennessee, by W Publishing Group, an imprint of Thomas Nelson.

Thomas Nelson titles may be purchased in bulk for educational, business, fund-raising, or sales promotional use. For information, please email SpecialMarkets@ThomasNelson.com.

Unless otherwise noted, Scripture quotations are taken from the Holy Bible, New International Version®, NIV®. © 1973, 1978, 1984, 2011 by Biblica, Inc.® Used by permission of Zondervan. All rights reserved worldwide.

Scripture quotations marked MSG are taken from THE MESSAGE. © 1993, 2002, 2018 by Eugene H. Peterson. Used by permission of NavPress. All rights reserved. Represented by Tyndale House Publishers, a Division of Tyndale House Ministries.

Scripture quotations marked ESV are taken from the ESV® Bible (The Holy Bible, English Standard Version®). © 2001 by Crossway, a publishing ministry of Good News Publishers. Used by permission. All rights reserved.

Scripture quotations marked NKJV are taken from the New King James Version®. © 1982 by Thomas Nelson. Used by permission. All rights reserved.

Scripture quotations marked NLT are taken from the Holy Bible, New Living Translation. © 1996, 2004, 2015 by Tyndale House Foundation. Used by permission of Tyndale House Ministries, Carol Stream, Illinois 60188. All rights reserved.

Scripture quotations marked CEV are taken from the Contemporary English Version. © 1991, 1992, 1995 by American Bible Society. Used by permission.

Scripture quotations marked NASB are taken from the New American Standard Bible® (NASB). © 1960, 1962, 1963, 1968, 1971, 1972, 1973, 1975, 1977, 1995 by The Lockman Foundation. Used by permission. www.Lockman.org

Any internet addresses, phone numbers, or company or product information printed in this book are offered as a resource and are not intended in any way to be or to imply an endorsement by Thomas Nelson, nor does Thomas Nelson vouch for the existence, content, or services of these sites, phone numbers, companies, or products beyond the life of this book.

ISBN 978-0-7852-5188-0 (eBook)

Library of Congress Cataloging-in-Publication Data

Names: Done, Dominic, author.
Title: Your longing has a name : come alive to the story you were made for / Dominic Done.
Description: Nashville, Tennessee : W Publishing Group, [2022] | Includes bibliographical references.
Identifiers: LCCN 2021053079 (print) | LCCN 2021053080 (ebook) | ISBN 9780785251705 (paperback) | ISBN 9780785251880 (ebook)
Subjects: LCSH: Vocation--Christianity. | Self-actualization (Psychology)--Religious aspects--Christianity.
Classification: LCC BV4740 .D68 2022 (print) | LCC BV4740 (ebook) | DDC 248.8/8--dc23/eng/20211130
LC record available at https://lccn.loc.gov/2021053079
LC ebook record available at https://lccn.loc.gov/2021053080

Printed in the United States of America

22 23 24 25 26 LSC 10 9 8 7 6 5 4 3 2 1

May the LORD cause you to flourish,
both you and your children.

PSALM 115:14

CONTENTS

LEAVE THE PARACHUTE

I recently read a story about the stuntman Luke Aikins, who made it into the *Guinness World Records* for—wait for it—jumping out of an airplane at twenty-five thousand feet *without* a parachute. Unfortunately, he died a few minutes later.

Just kidding.

He actually survived the unprecedented jump. How? Using GPS, he was able to navigate his 120-miles-per-hour plunge onto a massive ten-thousand-square-foot net that was suspended between four cranes. What the Associated Press reported is even more fascinating: "Just before climbing into a plane to make the jump, Aikins said he had been ordered to wear a parachute but indicated he wouldn't open it. As the plane was climbing to 25,000 feet above the drop zone he said the requirement had been lifted and he took off the chute." Aikins then leapt from the plane and for two minutes soared through the sky until, at the final possible second, he flipped onto his back and landed with seeming ease in the net.[1]

I don't know if I'll ever jump out of an airplane, but if I do, I'll probably ask for two parachutes. And a much, much bigger net.

That's why I'm in awe of Luke. If he had the parachute on him, even with the intention of not opening it, it wouldn't have been as compelling a story. Thousands of people with parachutes jump out of airplanes all the time. But the fact that he had none? Well, that's a story worth telling.

I'm even more in awe when I ponder the ruthless commitment that empowered him to leave the parachute behind. You don't just wake up one morning and decide to jump onto a net from the edge of space. Luke spent years and eighteen thousand skydives preparing. Before the stunt, which they dubbed "Heaven Sent," Luke and a team of scientists, physicists, and engineers designed a road map. They studied, read, meticulously built and tested the net, prepared the suit, analyzed the speed and direction of flight, and determined the exact position in which his body needed to be upon landing.

After they lowered him from the net, Luke was giddy with joy and the accomplishment of fulfilling his lifelong dream. He later wrote to his fans online: "My vision was always proper preparation and that if you train right you can make anything happen. Thank you!!!!"[2]

———

Anything of value exists as a consequence of what you put into it. Whether you're a skydiver, student, architect, or stay-at-home parent, the virtue you create in and through your life is intentional, not accidental.

The vital difference between soaring and splatting is *purpose.*

Nowhere is that truer than the deepest part of you: your soul. Intention washes from it the mud of ordinary life. The English novelist Daniel Defoe wrote of the soul's "luster,"[3] which, like a rough diamond, obtains its brilliance through deliberate care.

Luster. It's a word we don't often hear, but I think it's a good way to describe God's purpose for you—for your soul. It means *radiant beauty* or *splendor.* God's desire is for you—from the you that everyone sees to the you that is at your core—to flourish, grow, and prosper. He has a vision for you that is more dazzling and exhilarating than you could dare imagine: to embody his character, his nature, his beauty, his Son.

Right now this is what your soul is yearning to become. That longing you're feeling? It actually has a name: Jesus.

So how do you come alive to this vision?

It's likely not a good idea to leave the parachute behind and throw yourself headlong into the wild blue without preparation and a road map. The good news? There is a road map.

Buried in a chapter of the Bible that people rarely visit is a letter that Peter wrote to followers of Jesus who were aching for their souls to thrive. It was during a time, not unlike ours, of political and social unrest, racial tension, natural disasters, and a couple generations later, a pandemic. As you'll see, Peter's words are some of the most inspiring and soul-shaping insights ever written, and I'm convinced they're the exact message we need for the free fall we're all in.

Join me as together we examine seven gifts that, when practiced through the help of the Holy Spirit, will restore you, cause you to flourish, and even in difficult times, empower you to come alive to the story you were made for.

I.

STEP INTO THE STORY

God will still sing to you and call you by name into greater being and fullness of life. It will feel like longing.

—LISA COLÓN DELAY[1]

Late on a Tuesday evening in 2011, a columnist for the *Atlantic*, David Hajdu, was sitting in the Village Vanguard, a New York jazz club, doing some research on the city's music scene. The band launched into a song when a stylishly dressed trumpeter in an Italian-cut suit stepped forward and began a spectacular solo. Up to that point, he had been turned from the audience.

David Hajdu was stunned: *Is that Wynton Marsalis?*

How could the world's most renowned jazz musician, and the winner of nine Grammy Awards, be playing as a sideman in a hardly known band? And yet it was unmistakably him. Hajdu sat in the dark room, mesmerized as Marsalis's unique style, resonance, and breathtaking range stole the show.

The fourth song, a moody 1930s ballad called "I Don't Stand a Ghost of a Chance with You," featured another solo. Describing it as a "wrenching act of creative expression," Hajdu was spellbound as Marsalis not only played but also physically and emotionally embodied the spirit of the song. As he approached the end of the performance, his fingers sauntered fluently over every note. The crowd leaned forward eagerly.

Seconds before the most anticipated moment, the air charged with pent-up applause, someone's cell phone rang. It wasn't just an ordinary ring; it was an absurdly shrill, repetitive jingle that gets glued in your head. Awkwardness ensued as people turned to glare at the flustered offender. He quickly moved to silence the phone, but the damage was done.

Hajdu jotted in his notebook: "Magic, ruined."[2]

WHEN YOUR SOUL IS WEARY

Magic, ruined.

I can't help but think of those words when I reflect on the human experience and how our individual lives are often caught off guard by life's intrusions. We've all been there. Especially, it seems, over the last few years.

Disruption has come to us through a pandemic: the sting of grief and loss; trying to navigate work, school, and church via Zoom; racial, social, and political tension; global unrest and economic anxiety; not to mention the complex emotional struggles each of us has waded through. This has been a time of turmoil at every level, and our *souls* feel it.

Maybe for you, a relationship has been shattered because of a political disagreement, or a career you invested in for years dissolved because of budget cuts. An addiction you thought you'd buried suddenly reemerged during months of lockdown, or your trust in God has buckled under the weight of deconstruction. Whatever you're dealing with, there's no doubt that you join the overwhelming majority of us who now know what it's like when the magic is ruined.

Recent polls in the United States reveal how we're struggling physically, emotionally, spiritually, and mentally:

- 75 percent are overwhelmed by stress[3]
- 72 percent are exhausted[4]
- 68 percent feel defeated[5]
- 67 percent struggle with loneliness[6]
- 48 percent say they're hopeless[7]

The number of people who believe their lives are "thriving" has dropped to a low not seen since the Great Recession.[8] According to Harvard University, 51 percent of young Americans say they're discouraged. In the same survey, the majority describe having little energy, struggling with sleep, or finding "little pleasure in doing things."[9] It's almost like we're living NF's haunting song "I'll Keep On." Our souls are tired.

Maybe that's what's wrong.

Maybe what we're seeing and experiencing is a collective fatigue that goes well beyond whatever's happening out there; it's more like something *inside* us is broken. The spiritual writer Thomas Moore once said the "great malady" of the modern age is "loss of soul."[10] If true, that's a more harrowing diagnosis than you may realize. Your soul is everything. If your soul is flourishing, nothing you go through can destroy you. If your soul is crumbling, nothing you go through

THE HEALTH OF YOUR SOUL SHAPES THE OUTCOME OF YOUR LIFE.

can heal you. The health of your soul shapes the outcome of your life.

You'll know when something is wrong with your soul. How? It might manifest as negative thinking, restlessness, abrupt changes in emotion, an underlying sense of anxiety, disconnection from others, indifference, lack of aspiration, or burnout that no amount of sleep or time off can fix. A disordered soul is perpetually weary. In so many conversations lately, when I ask friends how they're really doing, they reply with a single word: *exhausted*.

Can you relate?

I'm not just talking about the kind of fatigue you have from staying up late, bingeing Netflix, or not having enough caramel macchiatos to jump-start your day. I'm talking about a soul-fatigue you endure in a visceral, all-of-life way. There is a kind of weariness that hits you in your gut: a gnawing, restless ache that tells you something is deeply wrong.

A recent article in the *New York Times* described our emotional state as "languishing." Languishing is a feeling of "stagnation and emptiness," the unshakable sense you're merely surviving instead of thriving.[11] Languishing is lostness. It's a lot like the German word *unheimlich*, or as the philosopher Heidegger put it, a profound sense of "not-being-at-home."[12] It's the restlessness that comes when you're lonely, adrift, or out of place. You might feel cold, numb, or indifferent; you scarcely remember the fire that once drove you to dream, risk, and step out.

A while back I had a chat with someone who was walking through a season of loss, which led to a crisis of faith. He admitted the problem wasn't that he felt too much but that he felt too *little*. His struggles had left him emotionally detached and spiritually disoriented.

"I just feel so empty."

As he continued to share, my heart went out to him. I recalled Jesus' invitation for the weary and burdened: "Come to me . . . for I am gentle and humble in heart, and you will find rest for your souls" (Matthew 11:28–29).

When Jesus promises *rest*, he doesn't mean a longer vacation, a lighter schedule, or a break from the office. He's speaking of a place where your inner life thrives and blooms with virtue. It's the possibility of green pastures and still waters that David foreshadowed in Psalm 23:3: "He restores my soul" (NKJV).

TO FLOURISH AGAIN

But how do we find such a life? Are these just poetic words, or a reality to step into? Can our souls be restored to flourishing again?

A simple prayer in the book of 3 John whispers *yes*: "Beloved, I pray that you may prosper in all things and be in health, just as your soul prospers" (verse 2 NKJV).

These words first struck me in 2020, when I found myself battling my own season of soul-fatigue. My family and I were living in Portland, Oregon, and I was doing my best to navigate our church through the pandemic—all while the region was rocked by violent riots, seething political tension, and historic wildfires that burned through vast parts of the state. It was one of the most discouraging seasons I'd ever gone through. Everywhere I turned, people were angry: angry about the virus, the election, shutdowns, social issues, injustice, the economy, protests, and Facebook posts.

Especially Facebook posts.

I met with people whose decades-long relationships had evaporated because of what others said online. They shared how toxic social media had become, how hurt they'd been by so-and-so's comments, and how alone they felt. Some joined virtual mobs, attacking, shaming, and canceling politicians or public figures. Others vented their anger on pastors and churches: attacking them for opening too soon, or not being open enough, requiring masks or not requiring masks, being too political, or not political enough.

I'm sure part of the angst emerged from sheer boredom. People were sick of being told what to do, sick of being stuck in their houses, sick of having to do school and work in front of a computer. Part of it also had to do with pent-up grief. As of September 2021, 72 percent of Americans say they know someone who was either killed or hospitalized during the pandemic.[13] In my extended family we lost several family members in a matter of months, including my mother-in-law, who died on Christmas.

Not long after, my wife suffered a spontaneous lung collapse. She spent several weeks in the hospital and months at home recovering. I remember one particularly intense day in the hospital just after her second operation to try to repair her lung. She woke up in excruciating pain. Every breath flooded her eyes with tears. I sat there helplessly, holding her hand, straining for the words to encourage her. But the truth was, at that moment, I didn't have much to give.

I felt so inadequate to handle everything that was being thrown at our family in that season. My wife's health. Our grief at losing her mother. Panic attacks. The pressures of work. At every turn there were disgruntled people. Night after night I struggled with insomnia as my mind raced: *God, what are you doing? Why are you allowing all of this? How do I overcome this discouragement?* Like an entropy of the soul, the more I grasped for answers, the more they eluded me.

One morning, after another restless night, I picked up my Bible and read those words in 3 John: *Beloved, I pray that you may prosper . . . just as your soul prospers.*

At first it seemed like a sarcastic joke. *Prosper? Really?*

My life, and the lives of so many other people I knew, felt anything but prosperous. *What does prospering even mean?* I wondered. I thought of the prosperity preachers on TV who insist God's purpose for our lives must be to make all our wildest dreams come true: Just rub the shiny lamp, buy the right books, say the right words or prayers, and presto! You'll drive a Tesla and date a supermodel, and your team will always win. Because God only wants you to be happy. *Right?*

If only. The coziest lies are the ones I want to believe.

I knew the verse had to mean something else.

I looked at it again, decided to do a little research, and discovered the word *prosper* has nothing to do with a better paycheck or a bigger 401(k). It means "to flourish." It's related to an old Greek phrase: "to help on the road."[14] John is revealing that God wants our souls to thrive at every point in our journey. Even the hard ones. Especially the hard ones. Because God's deepest work is not what he does *for* you but what he does *in* you.

True prospering isn't about escaping life's heartache, but rather encountering God's healing in the midst of heartache. That truth alone ought to reorient our perspective. Too often we'll pray for God to get us out of impossible situations. But sometimes God allows it to become *more* impossible so we can learn grit, vulnerability, and the fragile beauty of trust. And maybe then, once everything has been stripped away and nothing remains but God, we'll see the miraculous.

The verse filled me with hope. But it also lingered in my heart as a question: *What does that look like now, especially when my soul is so tired?*

John seems to suggest that soul-care is a step-by-step process, a road. And like any well-worn path, it offers growth, promise, and fresh perspective about self and God. But how do I get there?

Lord, how can my soul flourish?

That simple question sent me on a journey and a trajectory toward healing. Eventually, it led me to write the book you're holding.

I'm pretty sure God loves irony, though, because in no way have I figured this all out, not even close. I come to this book limping. But as we travel together, I'd like to share what I've learned so far. We'll explore seven gifts God has provided for our souls to flourish. They're based on an ancient path that was written about two thousand years ago in a relatively obscure letter: 2 Peter. The words aren't well-known, but never have they felt so fresh and timely. My prayer is that they will help encourage, inspire, restore, and heal you, as they have me.

YOUR INNER LONGING

Before we introduce the seven gifts, let's prepare for the journey with a salient truth: Flourishing flows from identity. If you want your soul to thrive, first accept who you are: passionately loved and relentlessly pursued by God. Then you can step into the story of who you were meant to be.

A surprising insight is found when we revisit the word *languish*. Its etymology goes back to a French expression, "to be faint," and even further back to the Latin *languere*, which is related to being "lovesick."[15] The idea is that although languishing may manifest superficially as malaise and complacency, deep down it unveils a soul crying out for love. As Shakespeare penned:

> Those lips that Love's own hand did make . . .
> To me that languish'd for her sake.[16]

8

Languish isn't the absence of emotion but rather the presence of longing. It's the ache of lovers, the sigh of weary travelers who yearn for home.

Why do I point this out? Because soul-weariness is often a symptom of *desire*. When you sift through the debris that's swirling in your life—past the grief, tears, disappointment, boredom, and frustration; past the confusion and apprehension about what tomorrow may bring—what you'll find is how fiercely lovesick you are for God. You burn with desire for more of his Spirit, his beauty, his redemptive nearness.

Identifying your soul's thirst for God creates space for your soul to flourish. Your longing has a name. And once you identify and name it, like anything meaningful in life, it shapes outcome. Your life dances to the music of your deepest love.

In Augustine's masterpiece *Confessions* he wrote: "My weight is my love. Wherever I am carried, my love is carrying me."[17] Augustine speaks of love as a force that lures us. So even as gravity pulls us toward itself, the soul incarnates what it loves. If the object of your love is anchored in the world, then you'll drift unmoored because your soul's infinite longing can only be satisfied by an infinite God. But when you're centered in God's love, his weight becomes your substance, his glory your delight, his essence the source of your flourishing.

You were made to live in radical intimacy with God. And everything within you affirms it.

When we get to chapter four, we'll unpack what this looks like practically. For now it's enough to acknowledge that what your heart craves is more of God. And here's the astonishing thing: Your lovesickness for God is only a faint echo of his lovesickness for you.

Remember how John began his prayer? *Beloved* . . .

The word *beloved* means "dearly loved." In the Old Testament, it's connected to the words *breath* and *longing*. God longs for you. His heart beats for you, languishes for you. He loves you with an intensity and unwavering persistence that defies imagination. Brennan Manning wrote in *The Ragamuffin Gospel*, "We should be astonished at the goodness of God, stunned that He should bother to call us by name, our mouths wide open at His love, bewildered that at this very moment we are standing on holy ground."[18]

This very moment.

Wherever you are, whatever your story looks like, your soul finds its identity in a God of endless love. That is the truest thing about you. You thought you had to find acceptance, but God had it all along.

THE PURSUING GOD

The beautiful surprise of pursuing God is the discovery that he is already pursuing you. This is a crucial revelation because too often we approach the subject of soul-health from a place of exclusion. Whether it's through podcasts, sermons, or well-intentioned books, we're frequently left with the impression that the primary barrier is *us*. We're told that because we're so flawed, the only way to flourish is to work harder: hire a life coach, spend a ton of money on seminars, adopt a series of disciplines, or realign our values to conceivably achieve our goals. Flourishing is thus presented as a far-off land for spiritual superheroes, and if we want to get there, we'll need to sweat.

There is a grain of truth here: Your soul demands cultivation and nurturing. But there is also *help on the road*. Do we have to work at it? Sure. More on that later. But the starting point of flourishing isn't exclusion; it's embrace. Flourishing isn't something you earn because you're driven. It's something you *receive* because you're loved.

The wayward prodigal son still had on tattered clothes when the father threw a party and welcomed him home. In the same way, God doesn't demand your performance but invites you to rest in his inexhaustible grace. He accepted you and called you "beloved" before you were even born. In Psalm 139:16 David voiced his wonder:

> You saw me. . . .
> . . . My life was recorded in
> your book.
> Every moment was laid out
> before a single day had passed (NLT).

FLOURISHING ISN'T SOMETHING YOU EARN BECAUSE YOU'RE DRIVEN. IT'S SOMETHING YOU *RECEIVE* BECAUSE YOU'RE LOVED.

If that's true, then flourishing isn't about trying to discover what's lost; it's rediscovering what's been there all along. God sees the finished you. The thriving you. The fully alive you. So the question is less "How can I morph into someone I'm not?" but instead "How can I live out God's vision of who I already am?"

As God sees it, you are:

- his child (John 1:12)
- his friend (John 15:15)
- his righteousness (2 Corinthians 5:21)
- his handiwork (Ephesians 2:10)
- his joy (Zephaniah 3:17)

- his delight (Psalm 18:19)
- his body (1 Corinthians 12:27)
- his bride (Revelation 21:9)

In a world that continuously lies about our identity, that loves to remind us of all we're *not*—not rich enough, smart enough, good-looking enough, or famous enough—God says: *You are mine. And you always have been. Nothing can change that.* You are not defined by the mistakes you've made but by the grace of God.

Accept you are accepted.

No mistake, regret, failure, weakness, missed opportunity, crippled hope, or season of discouragement can revoke the vision God has for you. In fact, I would argue that when the magic is ruined, it creates the conditions for transformation.

Your tears are not wasted. Every breakthrough begins with breaking.

Maybe your dreams were torn apart, maybe your faith was tested, maybe your strength was depleted; but rather than give up, you can reach into your soul and stand again. You have something to offer the world because that which is called cannot be silenced. You're still here. You're still trusting God. You still believe. Your life shouts that a wounded, limping faith is the most resilient and beautiful of all.

THIS THING CALLED GRACE

When my daughter, Amelia, was three years old, her favorite toy was Thomas the Tank Engine—the brash blue toy train with a perma-smile and a British accent. Remember him? My memories are still fresh from setting up train tracks that crisscrossed through the house, imitating the voices of his comrade coaches, and whisking Thomas to whatever adventure Amelia had in mind.

One day there was some serious drama between Amelia and Thomas. Exasperated, she threw him across the living room. Trying to seize a teachable moment, I put Thomas back on the track and picked up Amelia. "Honey, you should try to control your anger and not throw things. Because you did that, I'm going to give you a time-out." Amelia was devastated. She's always been an extrovert, and even as a toddler, a time-out was her version of emotional purgatory. She was desperate. She grasped my face and pulled me close with her little hands as we walked up the stairs to her room. Her vivid blue eyes were pleading.

"But Daddy," she implored. "What about grace? What about grace?"

I stopped in my own tracks and laughed. It was the ultimate catch 22 for a pastor. Every week I would preach about grace and invite people to receive it; but as we climbed the stairs, she called me out. What was I supposed to do?

Amelia never did get her time-out for throwing Thomas. We had a good talk, she apologized to her bedraggled train, and we continued playing. But I'll never forget those words about grace. And now, as a sixteen-year-old, she won't let me forget them.

We've all had our moments when the proverbial Thomas hits the wall. At least I have. But the grandeur of the gospel is this thing called grace. *Grace* is the word that describes the song in our heart when we find out we are loved. In the words of a timeless hymn, "Grace has brought me safe thus far, and grace will lead me home."[19]

But perhaps we can take it further. Because of grace, you're *already* home.

What do I mean?

Fasten your seat belt because this is mind-blowing. In the book of Ephesians, Paul described how God sees us: "Because of his great love for us, God, who is rich in mercy, made us alive with Christ even when we were dead in transgressions—it is by grace you have been saved. And God raised us up with Christ and seated us with him in the heavenly realms in Christ Jesus" (Ephesians 2:4–6).

Naturally, we assume verses like these are purely symbolic. Seated with him in the heavenly realms? *Isn't that when we die and go to heaven?*

Not so fast.

If you dig into the text, you'll find that Paul wasn't alluding to some day far off in the future; he was describing *now*. This moment, Paul insisted, you *are* seated with Jesus.

Wow! How is that possible?

There are a couple of ways to look at it. On one hand, from God's perspective, your journey is complete. You're already flourishing in his presence. This seems crazy until you realize God is outside of time. He sees the beginning, middle, and end of your life. The work is done. God isn't waiting around for you to fulfill your mission; from his vantage, you already have.

The nerdy part of me wonders if this could be interpreted through the lens of science. Physics tells us time is relative. Things such as light, gravity, and black holes can alter the flow of time. Furthermore, we're learning it's technically possible that parallel universes exist.[20] Cue the *Spider-Man* movies. According to this theory, another dimension could exist where you made better life choices, the pandemic didn't happen, America was united politically, and this book was written with nothing but text-speak. Clearly that's not the universe we inhabit, and luckily for you, I have an editor. LOL.

The point is, though, from a scientific perspective, it's not unthinkable that God sees reality quite differently from you. Right now, Paul said, you're seated with God—and in the first century, to be seated with a king was the highest honor imaginable.

When a hero conquered an enemy in war, he would return to a raucous celebration. People would flood the streets, shouting, singing, welcoming the soldier home. Then at the height of the event, with thousands looking on, the hero was invited to sit at the right hand of the king. Paul borrowed this ancient language to describe what God has done for us. Jesus, our hero, has defeated the enemy, overcome sin, and is seated at the right hand of God. But the plot twist, the scandalous surprise, is that he gives *us* the hero's welcome. He gives *us* the seat of honor. We did nothing while he did everything. The battle is won.

And if the battle is won, we are free from the pressure to perform. Your life isn't about striving for flourishing; it's about living from it. Christ in you is stronger than what's broken in you.

Could this be what Jesus meant when he said, "Your will be done, on earth as it is in heaven" (Matthew 6:10)? Those aren't just words to pray; they're a vision to chase after. Flourishing is about being on earth what God says is true about you in heaven. It's choosing to see yourself from God's eyes: his vision of you in the past, while you were still in your mother's womb; his vision of you in the future, seated in the heavenly realms, and asking: "How can I live this reality now?"

Before and beyond all time, God already accepted you. That means, in this momentary flicker we call life, this fleeting shadow between birth and death, literally nothing will separate you from his love.

> YOUR LIFE ISN'T ABOUT STRIVING FOR FLOURISHING; IT'S ABOUT LIVING FROM IT. CHRIST IN YOU IS STRONGER THAN WHAT'S BROKEN IN YOU.

As my daughter reminded me: There is grace. There always has been. There always will be.

Robert Farrar Capon, the late columnist, priest, and theologian, exclaimed:

Grace is the celebration of life, relentlessly hounding all the non-celebrants in the world. It is a floating, cosmic bash shouting its way through the streets of the universe, flinging the sweetness of its cassations to every window, pounding at every door in a hilarity beyond all liking and happening, until the prodigals come out at last and dance, and the elder brothers finally take their fingers out of their ears.[21]

Grace is not just forgiveness from your past. It's a way to live now.

THE MAGIC IS NEVER LOST

Remember the jazz club in New York City, Wynton Marsalis, and the crestfallen words of David Hajdu, the music journalist? He sat there, along with the distracted crowd, as the cell phone jingle stole the momentum of the ballad's magic moment.

But then something quite unexpected happened.

It only took a few moments, but as soon as Wynton unfroze, he lifted his trumpet and began to play, note for note, the melody of the ringtone. The audience cautiously laughed. Then he played it again, this time adding depth and intensity. Everyone leaned in once more. He carried on, now improvising, creating variations, changing notes—until slowly, masterfully, Wynton finished exactly where he left off with the line from "I Don't Stand a Ghost of a Chance with You."

The audience went wild. Just when everyone thought the magic was ruined, it had only begun.

Like Wynton Marsalis, true artists know how to create beauty from disruption. All the greats do. Frida Kahlo, an iconic female painter of last century, braved debilitating, lifelong pain. Martin Luther King Jr., while incarcerated in a narrow cell, wrote the masterpiece "Letter from Birmingham Jail." Banksy coats his provocative street art on dirty subway walls.

Any mime can duplicate that which exists, but a master creates something from nothing.

That's how I know you can flourish again. It's how I know your weary soul can find rest. Life may have made a wreck of you, but your Creator has only begun to reveal what he sees in you:

> No eye has seen, no ear has heard,
>   and no mind has imagined
> what God has prepared
>   for those who love him (1 Corinthians 2:9 NLT).

Of course, this kind of beauty takes *time*. It's why you must live it. The most meaningful things God does, he does slowly—in the secret, the stillness, when tomorrow seems veiled like a heavy curtain. Yet behind the scenes, God is setting the stage. He is apprenticing you now for your next adventure.

God knows how to take disenchanted people like you and me and compose a song.

And in many ways, he already has. You just need to learn its melody.

2.

TO BE FULLY ALIVE

May you follow the call of your soul, and may
you come to laugh with pure joy on the day your
deepest yearning becomes a reality.

—NAOMI LEVY[1]

On a shelf in my office I have a sealed jar that contains water I scooped out from a nearby stream. It's been there for years. Surprisingly, the water is still clear, but at the bottom lies a foreboding half-inch layer of sediment comprised of twigs, little stones, sand, dirt, and—if I were foolish enough to drink it—probably dysentery too. You would think after sitting for so long that maybe the sludge would consolidate or harden, but no. At even the slightest movement, the jar erupts into a swampy soup of debris.

Clarity, it seems, is a fragile thing.

I've kept the jar because it's a vivid reminder of our soul's palpable need for vision. We all long for a cloudless, lucid perspective of life: to know our purpose, our life's *why*, our reason for being. As Dostoevsky uttered, "The secret of man's being is not only to live but to have something to live for."[2]

But when you look around, and even more sobering, within, it's staggering how many of us live blurred lives: leaders who've lost their way and teeter on the brink of burnout, high school and college students who struggle with identity, exhausted coworkers who shuffle zombie-like through the day, friends who succumb to quick-fix addiction instead of processing their pain. Our soul's sense of calling, what the ancient Greeks called *telos*—or purpose—is noticeably opaque.

It wasn't meant to be like this. You weren't created to flounder in a place of unending weariness. Our bursting-with-joy God didn't speak you into existence so you'd live out your days with a depleted, gasping-for-air soul. He longs to "fill you with all joy and peace . . . so that you may overflow with hope by the power of the Holy Spirit" (Romans 15:13).

God's purpose for your life is that your soul would flourish. And when you open the pages of Scripture, you'll see this is true from day one.

IN GOD'S IMAGE

In the beginning, a beautiful God made a beautiful world teeming with wonder and possibility. Blue whales, zebras, snow leopards, hummingbirds, praying mantises, alpaca, and what I consider the pinnacle of his creation—Goldendoodles—bounded to life. Then, on the sixth day, God created the first humans: "Then God said, 'Let us make mankind in our image, in our likeness' . . . So God created mankind in his own image, in the image of God he created them; male and female he created them" (Genesis 1:26–27).

For years people have wrestled with these verses, not only because of how they describe creation but also because of how they describe God. For example, notice how God refers to himself:

Let *us* make . . .

Have you ever wondered, *Who is the* us? *And who is God talking to?* Some say God is conversing with the angels. Others say he's having his own inner dialogue or referring to himself like the Queen of England's royal *we*. But some leaders in the early church maintained the *us* is the first shout-out to the Trinity: the three-in-one Father, Son, and Spirit, each participating in creation. They called this moment *perichoresis*—which means to "dance around." It's closely related to the word *choreography*.

Think of the musicals *West Side Story* or *Hamilton*. There's an unspeakable magic when gifted actors dance, isn't there? You realize you're watching more than individual bodies; you're watching a harmonious set of relationships that move so effortlessly together they become a poetic blur. The universe, and all that's in it, is the poetry of God. It's the overture of a triune Being whose resonance pervades every molecule and atom.

It's no surprise, then, that the phrase *made in his image* is loaded with significance. Historically, there have been three ways of understanding it.

1. **RELATIONSHIP.** Even as parents desire to connect with their children, so, too, did God create us to have inseparable kinship with him.
2. **REPRESENTATION.** In former times, when kings ruled over their kingdoms, they erected statues of themselves to remind their

subjects of their protection and power. These "images" communicated to people, even thousands of miles away, that the king's rule was unimpeded by deserts, mountains, or oceans. To see an image was to experience the physical likeness of the king. So, too, as image-bearers of God, Adam and Eve mirrored his loving rule over creation by caring for the garden and its animals.

3. **QUALITIES.** The uniquely human capacities for self-awareness, rational thought, creativity, consciousness, and a thirst for worship flow from God himself.

When the Bible says you were made in God's image, it means you possess a desire to know and adore him and that he has gifted you with your personality, interests, and abilities to radiate his beauty in the world.

This description of our humanity, by the way, is what sets us apart from animals. Humans have a conscious awareness of the miracle and marvel of existence and an irrepressible yearning to whisper *thanks* to its Source. Animals, last time I checked, don't. Although, some might point out the difference between cats and dogs: A dog thinks, *My owners feed me, love me, pet me, and take care of me; they must be gods!* A cat thinks, *My owners feed me, love me, pet me, and take care of me; I must be a god!* Having owned both animals, I think that's pretty spot-on. But last I checked, even our Goldendoodle doesn't fold paws in worship before devouring her dinner.

There is something unique and exquisite in how God made *you*.

THE BEAUTIFUL MYSTERY OF WHO YOU ARE

Unlike the rest of creation, Adam and Eve didn't merely exist; they were ordained to live integrated lives with their Maker. In Genesis 2:7, we see how intimate this relationship was: "GOD formed Man out of dirt from the ground and blew into his nostrils the breath of life. The Man came alive—a living soul!" (MSG).

When you read the word *soul*, what do you think of? Defining it is more cumbersome than you'd imagine.

Atheists tell us there is no such thing as a soul, that all we're made of is physical atoms bouncing against each other in a universe that neither notices nor cares. The entertainment industry typically depicts the soul as something that keeps living when we die. Like those stories where someone expires on the operating table, and a ghost rises out of their body—or Disney's *Soul*, where a musician gets stuck in the afterlife with two-dimensional figures made of neon lines.

You'll often hear the word *soul* used for something you love or admire. Thus, you might say a band has soul, or a lover is your soul mate, or an athlete is the soul of a team, or a friend has an old soul. Sometimes people describe their emotional issues in terms of soul: "I feel like a lost soul" or "There's a hole in my soul."

Perhaps it's because of our convoluted definition of *soul* that we're unable to care for ours well—which is tragic because our souls are the symbiotic exposition of our entire being. For centuries, Jesus' followers understood that *soul* was far more than just an abstract notion disembodied from their earthly lives; it was essential to comprehending their selfhood. That's why when groups gathered in the 1800s for prayer or Bible study, their first question to one another was "How is it with your soul?"[3]

When God first created us, he envisioned flourishing—souls animated with his Spirit, breath, and presence. And how we embody that vision now has significance in eternity.

How does the Bible explain *soul*?[4] The simplest way to grasp it is *identity*. *Soul* is the essence of your being that brings together the

> *SOUL* IS THE ESSENCE OF YOUR BEING THAT BRINGS TOGETHER THE BEAUTIFUL MYSTERY OF WHO YOU ARE: YOUR PHYSICAL BODY, DESIRES, THOUGHTS, EMOTIONS, HOPES, AND PASSIONS.

beautiful mystery of who you are: your physical body, desires, thoughts, emotions, hopes, and passions. According to Dallas Willard, "The soul is that aspect of your whole being that *correlates*, *integrates*, and *enlivens* everything going on in the various dimensions of the self. It is the life-center of the human being."[5]

Notice the word *integrates*. This word comes from the Latin *integrare*, which means "to make whole."[6] Your soul brings together the entirety of what makes you, you.

In 1977 humanity made a valiant attempt to send the human soul into space. The Voyager 1 space probe was launched from Cape Canaveral, Florida, to begin a decades-long mission to explore the outer edges of our solar system. Scientists, in the hope that the ship would encounter alien life, placed on board an infamous Golden Record that featured sounds, greetings, images encoded in analog form, and an eclectic selection of music. As far as we know, the Golden Record never made it into the hands of aliens to motivate them to check us out—or if it did, perhaps they were scared off by seventies fashion. Still, it was a pretty creative way, as one journalist put it, to communicate "ephemeral evidence of the human soul."[7]

Your soul is the soundtrack of your life. Think of it as your Golden Record. Through the words you say and choose to dwell on, the habits you foster, the relationships you develop, the content you consume, and the decisions you make, you are forging your identity. Did you know that in any given day we make approximately thirty-five thousand conscious and subconscious decisions?[8] These range from what we eat (accounting for 226.7 decisions!) to what we purchase, to where we go online and who we'll spend our time with. Although each of these decisions may seem trivial in the moment, the power is in their compound effect. Choices accumulate, and over the course of life, they ultimately define you.

Your soul is the summation of your life choices. That's why the Bible incessantly warns us:

- "Take care, and keep your soul diligently" (Deuteronomy 4:9 ESV).
- "What good is it for someone to gain the whole world, yet forfeit their soul?" (Mark 8:36).
- "I pray that God, who gives peace, will make you completely holy. And may your spirit, soul, and body be kept healthy and faultless until our Lord Jesus Christ returns" (1 Thessalonians 5:23 CEV).

Notice how the last verse fuses together spirit, soul, and body. God wants to bring together *all* the elements of your life—your spirituality, physicality, emotions, sexuality, thoughts, choices, relationships, and desires—so you may live as a holy, whole, healthy, integrated person.

But when we bifurcate aspects of ourselves, separating what we do from who we are, the result is disintegration or unwholeness.

Perhaps that's a good way to describe sin. Soul integrates; sin disintegrates. Soul unites; sin divides. Sin is the unraveling of your soul's intricate unity; it defiles, corrupts, and poisons. Your soul breathes the secondhand smoke of your vices.

The reason God is against sin is because he's *for you*.

YOUR SOUL'S BREATH

In my early twenties, when I was a teacher on the remote islands of Vanuatu in the South Pacific, our water supply came from a catchment that sat at the bottom of a steep, corrugated tin roof. The climate of Vanuatu is wet and tropical, so with frequent downpours, water was readily available. I just needed to be sure the catchment stayed clean. One week, I learned this the hard way. Suddenly everyone at the school became violently ill. I still remember taking turns waiting for the "bathroom": a squalid hole in the ground, surrounded by bamboo for privacy. It was miserable! After days of enduring this, it finally dawned on me to check the catchment. I opened the lid slowly, dreading what I'd see. Sure enough, there was something floating inside: a large, abnormally waterlogged gecko that had swollen to two or three times his normal size. As I cringed at his unfortunate fate, I then knew the cause of ours: We had been living off gecko stew!

Kierkegaard's words are apropos here: "Sin grows every instant one does not get out of it."[9] Can you see why caring for our soul is so imperative? There is no greater resource that we must protect, honor, nourish, listen to, and safeguard.

And yet this irreplaceable treasure is what we so often neglect.

Some of us are too distracted to even notice how contaminated we are. And it's not just the obvious impulses of anger, greed, lust, fear, or jealousy that malform us. It's more insidious than that. Between juggling responsibilities at home, enduring drama at work, paying bills, fixing the car, checking notifications, doing chores, or changing diapers, we've become numb to the dynamics of our inner health. We also feel the reality of our made-from-dustness: physical exhaustion, emotional stress, and spiritual doubt, not to mention the menace of spiritual attack and the ongoing pressures of a consumeristic culture whose only goal is to consume us.

It's no wonder our souls are sick.

But God promises a path for us to heal.

In Genesis, when God created Adam, he *breathed* into him. Breathing on someone implies wordless intimacy. Think about it: If you're close enough to regularly feel someone's breath on your face, chances are you're already married to them or about to be! When God breathed, he filled Adam with his flourishing: his spirit, joy, grace, love, and beauty.

Your soul began as the breath of God. The implications are astonishing. First of all, it means the only way an unhealthy soul can be revived is through intimacy with him. When David wrote, "He restores my soul" (Psalm 23:3 NKJV), the original language meant "He will return my breath to me."

That's what we long for, isn't it? Our truest self is screaming for air, desperate to break through the surface of a shallow, hurried life and breathe deeply of God himself. To exhale failure and inhale grace. To come *alive* again. We'll unpack this more in chapter four.

Second—and most pertinent to this chapter—God's purpose for the first humans was much vaster than boring, superficial existence. He didn't manufacture them as soulless automatons or animals driven by instincts and urges; he conceived of

OUR TRUEST SELF IS SCREAMING FOR AIR, DESPERATE TO BREAK THROUGH THE SURFACE OF A SHALLOW, HURRIED LIFE AND BREATHE DEEPLY OF GOD HIMSELF.

living souls, sacred beings who were suffused, from their earliest gasp, with the Spirit's power.

The word *living* is semantically connected to *flourishing*. In fact, a verse after God breathed into Adam, the same Hebrew word is associated with the Bible's most common metaphor for the flourishing life: trees. In Latin, *flourishing* is translated "to be full of flowers." The image is of a soul blossoming with verdant color. And how could Adam not be? He had just inhaled God's breath. He was prospering and thriving; putting on display the words of Jesus, whom writers of the New Testament later called the second Adam: "I have come that they may have life, and have it to the full" (John 10:10).

That was, and always has been, God's purpose for humanity. And that was, and always has been, God's purpose for you.

Your soul was made to flourish.

WHAT IS FLOURISHING?

Okay, but what does flourishing *mean?* Well, like the word *soul*, it depends whom you ask. For most, flourishing has to do with "living the good life"—achievements or material success. A business is said to be flourishing if it's raking in a profit, or a social media account is flourishing if it has a ton of followers.

People sometimes use the word as a synonym for abundance or happiness, or the euphoria you get when you're in a place of "flow." In positive psychology, flourishing hinges on five attributes: favorable emotions, engagement, relationships, meaning, and accomplishments. One psychologist defines it as "the product of the pursuit and engagement of an authentic life that brings inner joy and happiness through meeting goals, being connected with life passions, and relishing in accomplishments."[10]

Notice how, by this definition, flourishing sounds like a "follow your bliss" cliché—contingent on rosy circumstances. But when the Bible talks about flourishing, it's rarely referring to accomplishments, possessions, or sappy optimism; it's talking about an inner virtue that grows despite how successful, or difficult, life may be. Scripture illustrates it with a trifecta of ancient words.

1. **SHALOM.** Found over two hundred times in the Bible, this word is usually rendered as "peace." We tend to view peace as the absence of conflict or a calm state of mind. It's what you feel after a glass of wine, an hour of yoga, or when your kids are finally asleep. But in the Bible, peace transcends life's circumstances. It's *inner* completeness, health, tranquility, rest, harmony, and joy.

2. **TAMIM.** This second word for flourishing means integrity, purpose, and singleness of focus. I think of an old friend of mine who moved to Vienna, Austria, to train for the Olympics. A uniquely talented volleyball player, he devoted years to perfecting his skills. I don't think I've met anyone more focused. He ate, drank, talked, slept, and dreamt volleyball. A few days before the competition, he sent me an email. The subject read "GOLD." Sure enough, in 2008, his team won, defeating Brazil in the final.

    If the email had been sent thousands of years ago, the subject line would have said *tamim*. *Tamim* is when you're so resolutely devoted to a cause that everything else fades from view. This razor-sharp devotion enables you to order your values, harness your energy, and prioritize your time.

3. **ASHREY.** This crucial word means "happy" or "blessed." It's used in Scripture to illustrate the joy that flows from a life firmly established in God. A lovely example is Psalm 1:1–3:

Blessed is the one
who does not walk in step with the wicked
or stand in the way that sinners take
or sit in the company of mockers,
but whose delight is in the law of the LORD,
and who meditates on his law day and night.
That person is like a tree planted by streams of water,
which yields its fruit in season
and whose leaf does not wither—
whatever they do prospers.

In this poem, David described the "blessed" (*ashrey*) life as a tree that's rooted in God and nourished from his Word. As a result, it's fruitful, flourishing, and whole. This synergy between the inner and outer self generates virtue that others both witness and benefit from.

In the Gospel of Matthew, Jesus used the Greek version of *ashrey* nine times in a segment of his sermon known as the Beatitudes:

Blessed are the poor in spirit . . .
Blessed are those who mourn . . .
Blessed are the meek . . .
Blessed are those who hunger and thirst for righteousness . . .
Blessed are the merciful . . .
Blessed are the pure in heart . . .
Blessed are the peacemakers . . .
Blessed are those who are persecuted because of
    righteousness. (Matthew 5:3–10)

Like David in Psalm 1, Jesus was portraying the blessed life. He was painting a picture of what it means to live integrated with God's rule and reign. Unlike some interpretations of this sermon, Jesus didn't intend these words to be a legalistic burden or religious obligation. He wasn't prescribing, he was *pronouncing*: the favor of God inhabits every step you take toward him.

Wait a minute. I can see why meekness, mercy, and peace are characteristics of blessing. But mourning? Persecution?

This is why Jesus' words are so subversive, at least by modern definitions of flourishing. He was saying the blessing of God is found not just beyond the pain, but within it. Even when you're flanked by heartache and sorrow, your soul can still thrive.

You can flourish regardless of what life throws at you.

ALL THINGS FOR THE GOOD

One of my favorite books is *A Severe Mercy* by Sheldon Vanauken. It chronicles the story of Vanauken and his wife, Davy. Through hours of resonant conversations, they quickly discovered their mutual affection for literature, dogs, travel, the sea, and art. It wasn't long before their friendship evolved into passionate love, commitment, and marriage. Although just nineteen years old, their love was like a "shining barrier" that shielded them from the unforeseen disruptions of married life: World War II, being uprooted from their home, tragedy, and sickness.

The most poignant test of their love, however, occurred when Davy surrendered herself fully to Jesus. Although Sheldon appreciated the role of faith in his life, Davy had a passion and fiery commitment he couldn't comprehend:

> Though I wouldn't have admitted it, even to myself, I didn't want
> God aboard. He was too heavy. I wanted Him approving from

a considerable distance. I didn't want to be thinking of Him. I wanted to be free . . . But for Davy, to live was Christ . . . His service was her freedom, her joy.[11]

She had unearthed a surprising paradox of the flourishing life: The truly free are bound in love. Shortly after her conversion, Davy was diagnosed with a rare virus and died a few months later. Much of *A Severe Mercy* focuses on Sheldon's journey of grief, acceptance, and personal awakening of the same resilient faith his wife enjoyed. Eventually, he dove headlong into pursuing God:

> The loss of Davy, after the intense sharing and closeness of the years, the loss and grief was, quite simply, the most immense thing I had ever known . . . I was driven by an unswerving determination to plumb the depths as well as to know the Davy I loved: to understand why she had lived and died, to learn from sorrow whatever it had to teach.[12]

Even in his pain, Sheldon experienced a renaissance of faith that caused his soul to flourish; it rushed through him with throbbing resolve. He came to recognize the fingerprints of God all over his life: in the joys and sorrows; the laughter and pain; the rapture of belonging; and the anxiety of loss. And God was there every step of the way, transforming him to be more like Jesus.

A well-known verse epitomizes Vanauken's journey: "And we know that in all things God works for the good of those who love him" (Romans 8:28).

Sadly, this verse is often misinterpreted to mean everything will work out *in our favor*. But when God says all things work for the good, he's describing a goodness much weightier than our comfort. Because

God is far more interested in changing you than your circumstances, the goodness he promises pertains to the virtue of the soul.

This is a far cry from the "good life" or guarantees to shield you from sorrow or keep you from pain; it's an invitation for your soul to flourish *even in the midst of pain*. That's why the very next verse says we are being molded "to the image of his Son."

God's purpose for your life isn't necessarily to make you wealthy, give you a bigger house, or make you TikTok-famous. His dream is that you become someone who reflects the image and beauty of his Son. Sometimes you'll hear people pray, "Make me like Jesus." But don't be surprised when the answer to that prayer resembles betrayal, pain, and crucifixion. The path to a resurrected, reborn self is forged in the shadow of the cross.

All things work for the good are gritty, raw, desperate words that speak to us with auspicious hope; despite every secret sorrow, tragedy, hostile person, stab in the back, unmet longing, season of grief, and disappointment, he desires to shape your soul to make you more Jesusy—forgiving, gracious, loving, contagious, joyful, and alive. As Jürgen Moltmann, one of the more astute theological minds of the last century, affirmed: "God weeps with us so that we may one day laugh with him."[13]

By allowing him to redeem our heartache, we can come alive to the story we were made for.

PARTICIPATION IN THE LIFE OF GOD

Shalom, *tamim*, and *ashrey* are magnificent words. But sometimes words are insufficient to convey the most meaningful moments in life. The birth of a child, the harmony and rhythms of music, a spring flower, a lover's kiss—such beyond-language encounters are difficult to explain yet incomprehensibly real to those who experience them.

Flourishing is something like that. That's why, in addition to using words, the Bible also paints pictures:

- *Flourishing* is a bountiful garden, Eden, with a Tree of Life in its center, blooming with goodness and beauty.
- *Flourishing* is Adam and Eve rooted there, living in soul-expanding intimacy with their Creator, breathing in his presence, implementing his mission in the world.
- *Flourishing* is the Bible's description of heaven: the tree of life replanted, a river gushing from the throne of God that reclaims a fallen world. Heaven is Eden restored (Revelation 21–22).
- *Flourishing* is the state of those who dwell there: the furnace of pain extinguished, every sorrow erased; mourning, sickness, disease, and war distant echoes of a broken past. Tears fade away, and all things are renewed.
- *Flourishing* is how Jesus lived: He loved his enemies, forgave his friends, ate with sinners, and chased after the banished and forgotten. He wandered through meadows and reflected how birds taught him not to worry; he withdrew to lonely mountains and told stories of shepherds with lost lambs in their arms. He broke his heart open in prayer and gave pieces of it away. The disenfranchised, marginalized, and oppressed found solace in his joy-soaked words, his touch, his compassion. He didn't withhold his love but furnished an empty world with its grace and power. No one who ever saw him walked away the same.
- *Flourishing* is how the Bible begins, it's how the Bible ends, and it's most spectacularly on display in Jesus. And he calls us to participate: "If anyone thirsts, let him come to me and drink.

Rivers of living water will brim and spill out of the depths of anyone who believes in me" (John 7:38 MSG).

It's here, I believe, that we arrive at our definition: *Flourishing is participation in the life of God.* It's finding your satisfaction, hope, and identity in him, and allowing his *shalom, ashrey,* and *tamim* to radiate from you. Flourishing is living like Jesus. It's so much more than self-focused feelings, you-be-you slogans, or trying to make your wildest dreams come true; it's knowing and being known by the One who breathed life into you. In him, you thrive. You're fully human. Fully the person he created you to be. Even as Adam and Eve were called to tend to the garden, so, too, our made-in-God's-image purpose is to tend to the garden of our souls.

FLOURISHING IS PARTICIPATION IN THE LIFE OF GOD.

Don't you long for this? Richard Foster wrote, "Don't you feel a tug, a yearning . . . ? Don't you long for something more? Doesn't every breath crave a deeper, fuller exposure to his Presence?"[14]

Even as I write these words, my soul resounds with an aching *yes!* I hunger for a life like that. I don't just want to hear about flourishing; I want to *encounter* it in the depths of my being, and bloom like the tree planted by rivers of water.

But, again, if I'm honest, I have *so* far to go.

The invitation into a "deeper, fuller exposure to his Presence" sounds amazing, but too often it's not my experience. If my soul was meant to be a glorious tree planted by clear streams, I feel more like a misshapen sapling with contorted, morose, fruitless limbs next to a dirty, gecko-infested pond. Even writing this book felt laughable at times. *Flourishing? Are you kidding me? I'm not even close.* Instead of *shalom*, what I often endure is anxiety. Instead of *tamim*, I clutter my life with distraction. Instead of *ashrey*, I struggle to see the blessing of God when life falls apart.

It's because I'm amply aware of my shortcomings that invitations like this seem impossible. *What's the point of trying today when I'll only fail tomorrow?* Flourishing seems like an unattainable ideal instead of a present reality.

If you can identify with this at all, let me share something with you that's been so liberating: *Flourishing isn't perfection. It's a process.*

I was reminded of this when I came across a short story written by J. R. R. Tolkien, who was a contemporary of Sheldon Vanauken. Tolkien once submitted a piece for the *Dublin Review* about a man called Niggle. Funny name, I know. It's about an artist who devoted himself to painting a tree. Niggle had a stunning vision in mind: He could see the world-weary hill on which the tree grew, its barrel-like trunk, the symmetry of every green, dewy leaf, and its heaven-pointing branches lifted high. He was passionate and determined to make it a masterpiece; he agonized over every detail but couldn't quite get it right.

Many years later Niggle journeyed hundreds of miles to a far-off country. And then, to his amazement one day, he saw on a distant hill an idyllic, radiant tree. He caught his breath. It was the exact tree he'd spent years trying to paint. But now, seeing it for himself, it was immeasurably more exquisite than he even imagined:

> He gazed at the Tree, and slowly lifted his arms and opened them wide.
> "It's a gift!" he cried.[15]

The tree is your soul. The destination is a masterpiece. But the pilgrimage to get there takes a lifetime.

You may look at your soul and feel frustrated, drained, and ready to give up. Maybe your soul is hurting because you just went through a breakup. Or a divorce. Your coworkers disappointed you. Your best friend turned on you. Maybe you're battling depression, lost a job or a loved one, or have been burned by the church. Or maybe all you see is how incomplete, immature, or imperfect you are.

Fear loves to remind you of how impossible the journey will be. Start anyway.

God meets you in the place of your deepest wounds and says, "My grace is enough." And he invites you to join him in cultivating the part of you that's longing to flourish: *your soul.*

Following Jesus isn't a quick fix. It's a journey: an invitation to learn and grow. It's a slow, aching, desperate-for-grace process of being shaped into the image of God. But the journey is why you're here. It's why he created you. It's how he sees you. And someday, in eternity, it's how you'll see yourself.

But until then, we step toward his beautiful vision.

3.

INTO THE DEEP

Keep looking at the bandaged place.
That's where the light enters you.

—RUMI[1]

Every journey needs a guide.

If you're about to learn a language, pick up an instrument, hone your skills in a career, or try a new sport, the best way to improve is to find someone who's done it—someone who's a step or two or ten ahead of you and can mentor you toward excellence.

It's fascinating how, in most areas of our lives, we freely seek help. ("Hey, Siri?") We'll reach for our phones to find the closest Chick-fil-A, to figure out what a Christopher Nolan movie means, or how to best season a steak. It's almost second nature to ask Google about anything. But when it comes to something as consequential as caring for our souls, we often wing it on our own.

Why is that?

Maybe it's hyper individualism; we're a nation of self-starters and bootstrappers, so we love to project the illusion we can do it alone. It could be that our culture idolizes physical bodies while disregarding vigilance for the unseen self. Or maybe it's because we intuitively know our souls are unhealthy, but we're too busy, afraid, or insecure to slow down and confront what's bruised inside. Peter Scazzero, exploring this question of identity, wrote in *Emotionally Healthy Spirituality*: "The vast majority of us go to our graves without knowing who we are."[2]

An outcome of having a mentor for the soul, however, is how that person helps us *discover* who we are. Seasoned leaders know the terrain of the interior life, and because they've made the journey themselves, they're atlases of experience and wisdom.

A famous Jewish rabbi once remarked: "Your house should be a meeting place for wise people. Attach yourself to the dust of their feet. And drink thirstily of their words."[3]

You're probably familiar with the idea of sitting at someone's feet to learn. Think of Mary, who sat at Jesus' feet (Luke 10:39), or Paul, who learned "at the feet of Gamaliel" (Acts 22:3 NKJV). In that culture, investing time at someone's feet was a posture of discipleship; you were there as an apprentice, to be educated and enlightened. You were powdered in their dust because as you trekked with them from village to village, hanging on their every word, the dust from their sandals covered you. You knew it was a good day if at the end you looked down and you were filthy.

When you came to know Jesus, you weren't just rescued from your old path; you were invited *into* a new spiritual journey. Jesus' first words to his disciples were: "Come, follow me" (Matthew 4:19). Following implies growth, change, learning, and giving space in our lives for God to refine and shape us until "Christ is formed in [us]" (Galatians 4:19). Every day is an opportunity to be covered in his dust.

This journey wasn't meant to be traveled alone, but rather with people who are dustier than you. Do you have someone like this in your life? A coach? A mentor? A pastor? A spiritual director? Like a garden, your soul can't flourish if there is no one to tend it. You need people who can roll up their sleeves, get their hands dirty, and dig into the thorny issues, hardened ground, and weed-infested patches you'd rather ignore.

Because God knows soul-care is arduous work, he gives us the gift of others. He also gives us the gift of his Word.

Every time you read the Bible, you're introduced to men and women who've gone before you and navigated dark and grueling seasons. They've battled weariness, discouragement, soul-numbing depression, and betrayal, but were sustained by God's unabating grace. The highs and lows of their lives are examples for us to learn from (Philippians 3:17).

For me, that dusty person is Peter. He was quite the colorful character: feisty, assertive, courageous, insecure, and notoriously unpredictable. One moment he was walking on water, and the next he was drowning. One moment he boldly declared Jesus was the Messiah, and the next he lectured Jesus for predicting the cross. Jesus' reply? "Get behind me, Satan" (Matthew 16:23). Can you imagine? Peter was doubtless called a lot of things in life, but Satan was a new low. Did you know Peter was the only disciple who was interrupted by the entire Trinity? It's true. (See also Matthew 17:5 and Acts 10:44.) Peter was the only one who denied he knew Jesus. But he was also the only one Jesus pursued to restore back to ministry (John 21).

Peter's journey of the soul is one of calling, near catastrophic burnout, and a slow migration toward flourishing. In his early days, people called him Simon. *Simon* means "to hear." Later he was given the name Peter, which means "rock." It's an interesting combination of names because Jesus once used these words in a parable to describe inner growth. He said the spiritually unformed person "hears" the word but does nothing with it. Their life is like someone who builds a house on sand. When winds and rain come, it collapses because it has no foundation. But the person who obeys God's Word builds a house on a rock. Even though the storms of life beat against it, the house endures because its foundation is robust (Matthew 7:24–27).

Every one of us is on a journey from Simon to Peter. It's a rigorous, humbling, and exhilarating path to walk, and we'll need all the help we can get. But that's why God gives us guides. Peter is wonderful to learn from because his life exemplifies that no matter how fractured our lives are, they can still become rocks. Look how far he came: he began as an exhausted, impetuous fisherman with an undeveloped soul, but he ended as a mature, Spirit-drenched disciple in a prison cell writing about seven ways our souls can flourish. That's quite the turnaround.

Let's sit at his feet awhile and see what we can learn.

PETER'S CALLING

Peter was nearly at his worst when he first met Jesus. After a long and sleepless night of fishing on the Sea of Galilee, his strength was depleted and his self-assurance shattered. Peter took pride in his ability to fish and feed his family, but that night he hadn't caught a single thing.

Then Jesus stood on the shore and called out: "Put out into deep water, and let down the nets for a catch."

Peter didn't take this advice well. He knew the trade and the lake like the back of his hand—and then a carpenter from *Nazareth* had the audacity to try to educate him? If a stranger has ever tried to tell you how to do your job, you know how irritating it is. You can hear the defensiveness in his voice: "We've worked hard all night." But then, a moment later, he relented: "Because you say so, I will let down the nets" (Luke 5:4–5).

There was something about Jesus that stirred longing inside the fisherman. Maybe it was how Jesus spoke, the joy shimmering from his face, or the sense of gravitas and presence he carried with him. Jesus seemed to embody an all-of-life flourishing that tugged on Peter's heart, beckoning him to reorient everything around his words. At his command, Peter, who had no practical reason to obey, took the boat into deeper waters.

But it wasn't easy.

After fishing all night, his muscles were screaming to rest. It was also humbling. The first-century historian Josephus recorded that hundreds of fishing boats would have been on the sea at any given time. It was a high-demand, highly competitive industry, and Peter had a reputation to defend.

Yet he mustered what little strength he had and forced his worn-out body to obey.

By the way, the surest sign God is about to do something deep inside you is when he calls you out of what's easy. God's vision for you isn't about comfort; it's about sculpting your character. Don't let security be your metric for discerning God's will. If it's of God, chances are it will look crazy.

DON'T LET SECURITY BE YOUR METRIC FOR DISCERNING GOD'S WILL. IF IT'S OF GOD, CHANCES ARE IT WILL LOOK CRAZY.

Put out into deep water . . .

Too often we're drawn to the placid currents. But any dead fish can go with the flow. God calls you upstream. He wants you to feel the rush of resistance. He wants you over your head because it's there your soul will thrive. What if, instead of making life easier, he wants to make it harder to teach you grit, trust, and the intimate beauty of all-or-nothing prayer? Jesus' healing feels a lot like pain. As Dietrich Bonhoeffer could attest, "Discipleship is not limited to what you can comprehend . . . Plunge into the deep waters beyond your own comprehension, and I will help you to comprehend even as I do."[4]

You weren't made for shallow waters; you were made for the depths. That's where you'll flourish. But to get there, you don't drift. You dive.

PETER'S FAILURE

From the moment Peter said yes to Jesus, and in the years that followed, Jesus never stopped urging him to go out further. He was constantly disrupting his complacency, speaking truth, challenging his assumptions, encouraging him to grow. It was excruciating at times, especially because Peter had some rough edges. His bulldozer personality was loud and abrasive, and he was known for having a foot-shaped mouth that got him in a lot of trouble.

But Jesus never gave up on him. Jesus was gentle, not judgy. He stood by Peter's side with a depth of solidarity and unfiltered kindness that gradually eroded his caustic edges.

Jesus pursued him and loved him, even at his darkest moments.

And none was darker than the night Jesus was betrayed, arrested, and condemned to be crucified. Terrified for their lives, every other disciple had fled, but Peter skulked in the high priest's courtyard and warmed himself by a fire. A servant girl approached him and said, "You also were with Jesus." Peter denied it. Another accused him of being a follower of Jesus. Yet, again, Peter denied it. Then others insisted, "Your accent gives you away." Maybe to prove his point, he began to curse. "I don't know the man!" (Matthew 26:69–74).

A rooster began to crow.

The verses that follow in Luke's account are some of the most haunting in all the Bible: "The Lord turned and looked straight at Peter. Then Peter remembered the word the Lord had spoken to him: 'Before the rooster crows today, you will disown me three times.' And he went outside and wept bitterly" (Luke 22:61–62).

Peter had done what he swore he'd never do: deny the One his soul loved.

But why? It's kind of surprising, isn't it? But, then again, it's always surprising when someone you thought was in a much better place flames out. Think of the people you assumed had it all together. Outwardly, they looked so moral and successful. And then you got a call, or you ran into someone at the store:

"Did you hear about so and so?"

"No. What happened?"

You stand there, blindsided, disbelieving as you hear yet another scandal, another betrayed marriage, another addiction, another person who did the unthinkable: "I never imagined he'd do that."

People can do such a good job of projecting what post-modern novelist Dave Eggers called "the ability to look, to the outside world, utterly serene and even cheerful," while, in our souls, all is "chaos."[5] Like lava breaching a thin surface, a disordered soul inevitably erupts its pain; and the aftermath is ruinous: burned-out lives, broken homes, scorched relationships.

Peter Wept

The word *wept* means to sob violently. Peter came face-to-face with his shadow side, and it broke him. He thought he was so much stronger than that. How did he get there?

Was it just a spell of weakness, or was there ongoing sin in his life? Was he disillusioned by Jesus' arrest? Was he harboring resentment? Perhaps it was a failure to pray. I've always found that prayer is an accurate barometer for my soul's health. If I'm living in rooted dependence on God, my soul expresses its longing through words. But if I've become entitled or proud, the first thing to go is intimacy with God. Prayer cannot exist with ego. And vice versa.

Personally, I think Peter was just exhausted.

We already know he was unable to stay awake in the garden of Gethsemane. For three years, he followed Jesus as they sojourned through dusty Galilean roads casting out demons, touching lepers, and preaching the kingdom—and dealing with disgruntled disciples, fuming Pharisees, and imperious Roman soldiers. Now his strength was sapped, and his soul was weary.

In a moment when the majority of us rarely feel rested, Peter's exhaustion is a timely warning—sometimes the most urgent need for our souls is physical rest.[6] Theologian D. A. Carson underscored the profound interconnection our physicality has on our interior life:

> We are whole, complicated beings; our physical existence is tied to our spiritual well-being, to our mental outlook, to our relationships with others, including our relationship with God. Sometimes the godliest thing you can do in the universe is get a good night's sleep.[7]

Whatever brokenness lurked underneath the surface of Peter's life, Jesus, as always, met it with compassion. Hurting people don't need critics. They need a refuge. Jesus turned and "looked" at him. I used to think this was a look of judgment, disappointment, or anger. Kind of like when you were a kid and your mom gave you "the look" to get you to behave. Yet the intention was anything but harsh. It was a gaze of tenderness—how someone looks at their friend with sympathy when they're struggling with grief. Intriguingly, the word *looked* here is the same word found earlier in the Gospels when Jesus first called Peter and gave him his name.

HURTING PEOPLE DON'T NEED CRITICS. THEY NEED A REFUGE.

With a single glance, Jesus was reminding him of his worth and identity. He may have failed, but from Jesus' perspective, Peter was still a rock. He was still accepted. He was still called. His soul could flourish again.

It's been said that a saint is "not someone who is good but who experiences the goodness of God."[8] That defines Peter's story. As the years passed, and he grew older, the dust of his Rabbi gradually covered him. He became gentler. Kinder. Wiser. More gracious and humble. In the book of Acts, the Spirit ignited his heart, and in the very same city where he denied Jesus before a smoldering fire, he spoke with conviction to thousands and later led a church that was planted there.

The failed fisherman had become a fisher of men.

It's not how we start that determines our ending; it's what we allow the Spirit of God to do in between. Although the journey to get there was slow and winding, Peter's soul gradually healed as he embraced the life God had for him.

PETER'S WISDOM

Years later, when Peter was in his sixties, a fire suddenly broke out among the merchant shops lining the Circus Maximus. The Circus Maximus was the largest stadium in ancient Rome that was built for mass entertainment, fights, animal hunts, and chariot racing. (If you've seen the movie *Gladiator*, think of the scene where Maximus, played by a brawny Russell Crowe, stares down the sadistic emperor.) The fire spread quickly, and within nine days, two-thirds of Rome had been destroyed.

At that time Nero was ruling, and according to the Roman historian Tacitus,[9] he used the tragedy to scapegoat Christians and marginalize their influence. He began rounding them up, torturing and publicly executing them. Christians lost their lives and their livelihoods. Many fled the city. Many more went underground to escape Nero's tyranny.

Peter was arrested and jailed. He knew his chances of survival were slim, but he wanted to encourage his fellow disciples anyway. They needed hope and were desperate to know how their souls could flourish in difficult times.

So, as he languished inside a prison cell, he picked up a pen and wrote:[10]

Simon Peter, a servant and apostle of Jesus Christ,

To those who through the righteousness of our God and Savior Jesus Christ have received a faith as precious as ours:

Grace and peace be yours in abundance through the knowledge of God and of Jesus our Lord. His divine power has given us everything we need for a godly life through our knowledge of him who called us by his own glory and goodness. Through these he has given us his very great and precious promises, so that through them you may participate in the divine nature, having escaped the corruption in the world caused by evil desires. (2 Peter 1:1–4)

Notice how flourishing imbues Peter's every word: *grace and peace in abundance, divine power, glory, goodness, great and precious promises, everything we need.* When you consider the bleak backdrop of his circumstances and the trauma the Christians of his time were experiencing, the colors Peter painted with are a stunning contrast. But maybe that's the point. Peter was reminding his brothers and sisters that their souls could prosper, even when their world was caving in.

A few verses later he added: "Make every effort to confirm your calling and election" (2 Peter 1:10).

The word *calling* is fascinating. It was sometimes used in the ancient world to describe someone being summoned to an opulent feast. If you were a peasant, imagine what an honor that would have been, especially if the meal happened to be with a king.

I once had the opportunity to go to Belgium to attend a breakfast with politicians and leaders from across Europe. My friend who invited me began introducing me to impeccably dressed dignitaries, some from royal families. We enjoyed meals, listened to engaging speakers, and heard updates from their countries. It was an incredible time. I was so grateful to be in the room, but I couldn't shake the feeling that I was seriously out of my depth. *What am I doing here? I'm a nobody pastor!* The whole time, people were chatting with me as if I belonged. "So what nation do you lead?" they asked. Ha! It was surreal.

Peter let us know we're invited, in our weariness and ordinariness, before an extraordinary King. It's uncomfortable at first because we know we don't deserve to be there, but our Host smiles anyway and hands us broken bread and a cup of wine.

A Way to Thrive

Peter, too, was once given bread and wine by a King. And now, in his waning hours, he shared the same hope he once received: God has a calling on your life. He loves you. He longs for you. He has prepared a feast, a table for you in the presence of your enemies.

Peter wanted the struggling church to know that when life is blowing up, when the enemy is besieging and all hell is breaking loose, there is a way to thrive. There is a way to enjoy the extravagant feast, to experience the glory, the goodness, the great and precious promises.

And here's how:

> Make every effort to add to your faith goodness; and to goodness, knowledge; and to knowledge, self-control; and to self-control, perseverance; and to perseverance, godliness; and to godliness, mutual affection; and to mutual affection, love. (2 Peter 1:5–7)

For years I assumed this was simply a list of descriptive virtues, like those you see throughout Scripture, such as "the fruit of the Spirit" (Galatians 5:22–23) or "the wisdom that comes from heaven" (James 3:17–18). But during my own season of loss, discouragement, and exhaustion, I read it again. And again.

It hit me.

Peter's words don't just define what a wise, spirit-drenched life ought to look like. Nor are they just another list of spiritual habits or disciplines we're obligated to implement in order to be blessed. (Although, as we'll see later, we *are* called to practice them). As I dug into the verses, and especially the context where Peter described the lavish generosity of God, I realized these seven virtues aren't only duties to perform but gifts to receive. Like liturgy for a weary soul, they're intended to heal and pivot our lives back toward its center in the life of God. As we add them to our faith, one upon another, our souls are empowered to flourish. As Peter promised, "If you possess these qualities in increasing measure, they will keep you from being ineffective and unproductive" (2 Peter 1:8).

Ineffective and *unproductive* are two ancient words that were used to describe a tree that was withering on the inside and had lost its ability to grow fruit. Having been there and endured periods where his own soul atrophied but then, by God's grace, began to blossom, Peter announced an astounding promise: *Your soul can live again.*

GOD'S WILL FOR YOUR LIFE

These seven gifts, with Peter as our guide, have the capacity to rehabilitate and restore the deepest part of you. As we journey through the book, we'll unpack each one together. But first, notice how Peter set it up: *Add to your faith.*

Add *what* to your faith?

He didn't tell us to add things that are skin-deep or artificial. Instead, Peter focused on the formation of the soul: *goodness, knowledge, self-control, perseverance, godliness, mutual affection,* and *love.*

Why did Peter start there? Because God's will for your life is not about what you do but who you *are.* You were created to "take on an entirely new way of life—a God-fashioned life, a life renewed from the inside and working itself into your conduct as God accurately reproduces his character in you" (Ephesians 4:22–24 MSG).

This explains why virtually every time you see the phrase "the will of God" in the Bible it is framed in terms of becoming a God-reflecting human being. For example, God calls us to:

- be holy (1 Thessalonians 4:3)
- live honorable lives (1 Peter 2:15)
- pray and practice gratitude (1 Thessalonians 5:17–18)
- walk in wisdom and be full of the Spirit (Ephesians 5:15–18)
- have renewed minds and surrendered lives (Romans 12:1–2)
- live worthy of the Lord (Colossians 1:9–10)

In all of these verses and many more, God's will is defined as the hidden work of refining, growing, maturing, and chipping away at the old self in order to remake us into the new, Jesus-mirroring self.

This is counterintuitive because when we raise questions about God's will, we typically assume it has to do with life's details: Should I take that position at work? Should I break up with that person? Should I major in that degree? Should I move to that city? Whenever Scripture speaks about the "will of God," however, it's rarely describing the decisions we make; instead, it's casting a vision for the person we ought to become. Until the vast chasm that is our inner life has yielded to the way of Jesus, we are powerless to wisely navigate the complexities of our outer life.

I love how N. T. Wright described life's purpose:

UNTIL THE VAST CHASM THAT IS OUR INNER LIFE HAS YIELDED TO THE WAY OF JESUS, WE ARE POWERLESS TO WISELY NAVIGATE THE COMPLEXITIES OF OUR OUTER LIFE.

The goal you are meant to be aiming at once you have come to faith, the goal which is within reach even in the present life, anticipating the final life to come—is the life of fully formed, fully flourishing Christian character.[11]

You might ask, "What should I do with all the decisions I still need to make? How do I navigate the details of my life wisely?" Here's the wonderful truth: the more you're covered in the dust of your Rabbi, the more you'll be able to distinguish what the next step should be. The famous architect Louis Sullivan once remarked that when building a structure, "Form follows function." That is to say, the shape of the building ought to reflect the *purpose* for which it was designed. So, too, when we build our lives using the blueprint of Jesus, the details of life instinctively unfold. That doesn't mean the details aren't important; they're just a distant second to your central calling.

Here's an illustration that will require a lot of imagination—especially if you're a parent. Let's say your middle schooler suddenly announces: "Mom, I really want to help you clean! Can I please vacuum the house?" After you recover from your heart attack, you express how grateful you are: "Wow. That's great, honey, thank you!" But then, imagine your child anxiously rushing up to you five minutes later: "Help! I don't know where to begin! Where should I start?" You probably smile and reply that it doesn't matter: "Any room will do!" You're just grateful for their newfound mania for cleaning and even more grateful they're developing selfless character. As a parent, your primary goal is for your child to become godly, discerning, and wise. The room is irrelevant. Even how well they clean doesn't matter. What matters is the heart.

As children of God, we sometimes get too hung up and anxious over life's options: *How do I know this is the right job? House? City?*

Church? Program? Again, it's not that those questions don't matter, but I often wonder if God smiles as a parent would and says: "Start anywhere! I'm just glad you're my child."

This world is God's house; and time is fleeting, so enjoy it. Have fun! "Delight in the LORD, and he will give you the desires of your heart" (Psalm 37:4). Work on being the right person, and then go where your most beautiful prayers take you.

Ask where God is moving, then join him there.

DEEP GLADNESS. DEEP HUNGER.

As you begin the journey, remember that God's invitation for the flourishing life is not just for our own sake; it's for the flourishing of *others* too. Again, think of David's tree in Psalm 1:3; the further your roots go into the heart of God, the more fruit will burst out of you. It's inevitable. Your heart, like Jesus, will naturally scatter *shalom* everywhere you go. As Frederick Buechner explained, God wants you to thrive so that you can be a blessing to others: "The place God calls you is the place where your deep gladness and the world's deep hunger meet."[12]

What is your deep gladness? What makes you come alive? What tugs at your heart and makes you think, *I was made for this*?

For you, what is the world's deep hunger? Where do you see the greatest needs? What keeps you up at night? What makes you livid? Child abuse? Racism? Poverty? Sex trafficking? Animal extinction? Lack of access to education in developing countries? Name the thing that ignites your heart to burn for justice. Because what you name is what your faith yearns to act on. As the public intellectual Miroslav Volf described: "Faith is an expression of the fact that we exist so that the infinite God can dwell in us and work through us for the well-being of the whole creation."[13]

Your faith will become sight, your soul will flourish, and your character will look most like Jesus in the place where your gladness and the world's needs collide. And when you read the Gospels, isn't that how Jesus did life? His heart throbbed for the sick and lonely. He pursued the disenfranchised, disillusioned, and displaced, and he had no greater joy than welcoming them home.

In Luke 15, the Pharisees criticized Jesus because of this, and so, as he loved to do, he told them a story. There was a woman, he said, who lost 10 percent of her life's savings. Understandably, she panicked. She tore the house apart, sweeping floors, hunting under tables, moving couches. After hours of frantic cleaning, she was reunited with her missing coin. She was so relieved she called her neighbors for an impromptu party. In Jewish culture, parties aren't stoic affairs; they're rowdy, exuberant, and loud. People began spilling into her home, laughing, eating, drinking, taking selfies at the photo booth, and lining up at the food trucks in the driveway. They were ecstatic because what was lost had been found (verses 8–10).

The flourishing life looks a lot like that heartsick woman. Something detonates in your heart and sets fire to your bones. It gets you out of bed in the morning, makes you ransack houses, call up your friends, and throw all-night parties.

Flourishing is deep gladness. It's also deep hunger. It's what Jesus looks like in flesh and blood: materializing his love, grace, and passion for the heartsick and spiritually homeless.

It's being his hands, feet, and healing presence on a planet that knows only oppression, anger, and fear.

It's seeing what's lost and showing up there.

It's radiating Jesus' beauty to all that's twisted around us.

It's sowing new creation within the chaos of the old.

Calling is *your* part in the mission of God.

Seen this way, God's will is far simpler than we ever could imagine. We don't have to overthink it. Just follow Jesus, and let his dust cover you.

Like Peter, this is the flourishing your soul craves—to sit at Jesus' feet; to be his image-bearer, coin-finder, party-thrower, hope-bringer; beaming his joy into the world.

4.

BREATHE AGAIN

Add to your faith goodness.

—2 PETER 1:5

I once read a hilarious true story out of Kenansville, North Carolina, about a sixty-seven-pound, one-year-old lab who began stealing from a local Dollar General store. His target? A purple unicorn he was infatuated with. Waiting outside, he ran in whenever the doors opened, dashed to the toy aisle in the back, grabbed the same unicorn in his mouth, and then tried to escape. The employees repeatedly had to chase the dog down, rescue the bedraggled unicorn, and put it back on the shelf. The dog didn't give up. For several days, he kept sneaking back inside and making off with it, only to be caught over and over. Finally, the owners called animal control. The officer who came to capture him was so moved by his boundless dedication that she paid the ten dollars for the purple toy before bringing the dog—whom they named Sisu after the movie *Raya and the Last Dragon*—and his unicorn to a shelter. A day later, Sisu was adopted, and now there are pictures all over the internet (check them out; they're adorable!) of the dog who moved heaven and earth just to be with his beloved.[1]

You've got to admire him for that.

Have you ever wanted something so bad you'd do almost anything to make it a reality? A business strategy? A dream you can't shake? A relationship? Who knows, maybe you're all about purple unicorns too.

We have a word for that—*resolve*—which is actually the Greek word Peter led with as he invited our souls to flourish: "Make every effort [resolve] to add to your faith" (2 Peter 1:5). Peter was urging us to do everything in our power to attend to our inner life. Because, as we explored in chapter 2, nothing is more valuable: "Watch over your heart with all diligence, for from it flow the springs of life" (Proverbs 4:23 NASB).

You can lose part of your body, or have an organ transplant, and you'll still be alive. But if you lose your soul, you've lost everything. Your soul is the fulcrum of your identity, imagination, creativity—of *you*. Think of the accomplishments you're proud of: painting a work of art, restoring an old car, saving up to surprise your spouse with a romantic gift or getaway, or writing a poem or song. Those things didn't just magically appear; they came from your *soul*. Anything beautiful you achieve in the world emanates from your soul. Anything you're ashamed of also emanates from your soul.

> ANYTHING BEAUTIFUL YOU ACHIEVE IN THE WORLD EMANATES FROM YOUR SOUL. ANYTHING YOU'RE ASHAMED OF ALSO EMANATES FROM YOUR SOUL.

That's why Peter insisted: *Make every effort. Resolve.*

Soul-care isn't an optional if-you-have-time-for-it luxury. It's essential. Your soul is your lifeblood. All that you are rises or falls on its health. God, who is passionately in love with you, who created you and gave you your soul, invites you—no, pleads with you—to steward it. That's why these verses in 2 Peter exist. They're not just another collection of words to read past; they're a necessary road map for thriving.

BEGIN WITH GOODNESS

As we've seen, the seven gifts God provides for a flourishing life are: goodness, knowledge, self-control, perseverance, godliness, mutual affection, and love.

But let's start with the first: *add to your faith goodness.*

Goodness. That clears things up, right? Not really. Talk about a broad, hard-to-define word. We use "good" in so many contexts: Someone asks how you're doing, and 99 percent of the time, you'll say, "I'm good." You may or may not be, but it's usually a polite excuse to bow out of a conversation. Or we'll say we "feel good" because we spent time at the gym, went for a hike, or had our sixth cup of coffee. Or we'll call our boss "a good person" because he just gave us a raise at work.

But when Peter used the word *good*, he wasn't just giving us a placeholder to describe something we like; he was uncovering the bedrock of flourishing. *Goodness* is the foundation of all the other virtues, with each successive virtue built on the one before. That's why he repeated himself after every word—"add to your faith goodness; and to goodness, knowledge; and to knowledge, self-control . . ."

But what does *goodness* mean?

First, let's revisit the Greco-Roman world to see how they understood *goodness*. They called it *árete*, which means "excellence." A house was considered *arete* if it was comfortable and well-designed. Food was *arete* if the taste, texture, and aroma was mouthwatering. In Homer's epic poems, the *Iliad* and the *Odyssey, arete* was the word to describe the aristocracy and warriors who were strong, intrepid, and unusually skilled at fighting. Those with *arete* were assumed to be the privileged of society: smart, disciplined, good looking, wealthy, well educated, and well connected. And if they lacked those things, they needed to try harder, work more, and get better friends or a better education. *Arete* was a by-product of human effort and discipline, and a little bit of luck too. In fact, in a sexist Greek culture,[2] many of the male philosophers articulated that *arete* was out of reach for women, who were afforded fewer rights than men.

The writers of the Bible, however, had an entirely different vision. Goodness wasn't just something you achieved through gender, luck, or exertion; it was something you received through *relationship with God*. Psalm 34:8 reads, "Taste and see that the LORD is good; blessed is the one who takes refuge in him." Remember, *blessed* is that beautiful word *ashrey* (or flourishing). Why do those who run to God flourish? Not because of their own excellence or efforts but because they're sheltering in him.

Prayer is how God's goodness flows into us. I think of Acts 4:13. The religious elite were stunned that Peter and his friend John were so courageous. They didn't meet cultural expectations; they didn't have the "right" background, looks, or education. They were *ordinary* men. So what made them courageous? *They had been with Jesus.* That's the key.

Unlike the Greek worldview, goodness isn't about how far you go in life; it's about how deeply connected you are to God. Your life could be in shambles right now. You might be struggling with your health, debt, a crisis, or a difficult decision. You might be unpopular or failing at the social media game. You could be losing at every possible metric that culture defines as *success*, but if you're in love with Jesus and centering your life around him, you are forging a life of depth and substance. You are becoming a person of *arete*.

THE GOODNESS OF GOD

A noteworthy illustration of *arete* is found in Exodus 32–33. After freeing the children of Israel from their slavery in Egypt, God led them past armies and through the Red Sea with Moses as their appointed leader. When Moses brought them to the base of Mount Sinai, he climbed the mountain, where he received from God ten commands engraved in stone tablets, only to return and find the Israelites naked and dancing around a calf they had fashioned out of gold. To demonstrate how they had already violated God's commands, Moses dramatically threw down the tablets, which shattered at the base of the mountain.

With a heavy heart, Moses trudged back up Sinai, only to be met with a promise from God: "I will cause all my goodness to pass in front of you, and I will proclaim my name" (33:19). In the Bible, a person's *name* was often indicative of their reputation (think Abraham, Sarah, Jacob, or Peter). But here, God wanted Moses to know who *he* was: goodness. Goodness and God's name are one and the same.

As seen throughout the Bible, God is goodness personified:

- "Give thanks to the LORD, for he is good" (1 Chronicles 16:34).
- "Good and upright is the LORD" (Psalm 25:8).
- "The LORD is good to all" (Psalm 145:9).
- "No one is good—except God" (Mark 10:18).
- "God is good" (Psalm 73:1).
- "You are good, and what you do is good" (Psalm 119:68).

From the opening lines of Genesis, where God pronounced his creation "good," to the final book of Revelation, where he restores goodness to a creation that had become corrupt, virtually every page of the Bible characterizes God as the standard and wellspring of *good*: *Moses, I want you to know who I am—not just theoretically but intimately. I want you to gaze on me and see what goodness looks like* (Exodus 33:19).

A few verses later, as Moses crouched behind the rock, God walked by. It was such an intense experience that God had to shield Moses with his hand (Exodus 33:20–23). Even then, Moses' face began to glow and shine, physically radiating the brilliance of what he had just seen. For the people below, it was too much. When he returned, they made him put on a veil (Exodus 34:29–35). Moses had been with God; and like a bottle of soda after a hard shake, goodness was erupting out of him.

God's goodness is so much a part of his being that it doesn't just exist inside of him; it overflows. There is complete harmony between who God is and what God does. So when you align your life toward him, you can't help but come off the mountain like Moses: beaming with life. As Mother Teresa expressed, "Prayer enlarges the heart until it is capable of containing God's gift of Himself."[3]

Can you see why Peter began with this gift? It is the basis of all seven; the foundation of our flourishing. And goodness is added to our faith when, like Moses, we open our hearts to intimacy with God.

DRAWING FROM THE SOURCE

If there's one thing I'd love you to take away from this book, it's this: In order to flourish, your soul needs to be drawing from the source of flourishing, God himself.

Jesus said, "Abide in Me, and I in you" (John 15:4 NKJV).

Abide means to "make your home with," or "remain" in unguarded friendship. Just as you relax and let down your hair with your closest friends, the kind of relationship Jesus desires is nothing-to-hide familiarity and fellowship. In my years as a pastor, I was often invited to people's houses for dinner. I remember one time showing up early and hearing an Eminem song laced with F-bombs blaring from the other side of the door. I knocked. Seconds later I could hear they had changed the playlist to Hillsong! Chaos ensued: "Quick! Throw that bottle in the closet! The pastor's here!" If only people knew that most pastors aren't that uptight. We've seen it all. But I still thought it was funny.

Abide calls us to live openly and transparently with Jesus. There are no secret closets, nothing to hide. The door is flung wide, and he is fully at home in every area of our lives: in our habits, finances, relationships, in how we speak, what we listen to, and where we go online. He wants his goodness to fill every nook and cranny of our souls.

This goes far beyond the oft-heard cliché about prayer: "Spend time with the Lord," which implies that all he wants is a few minutes of our busy schedule. True discipleship isn't about giving God your leftovers; it's all-of-life surrender to King Jesus.

Perhaps that's what Paul meant when he crisply penned, "Pray continually" (1 Thessalonians 5:17). If you recall, a couple chapters ago we saw how this verse was part of the list of verses defining God's will for our lives. There's a reason for that. The life we shape tomorrow is forged by the words

TRUE DISCIPLESHIP ISN'T ABOUT GIVING GOD YOUR LEFTOVERS; IT'S ALL-OF-LIFE SURRENDER TO KING JESUS.

we pray today. When we yield our all, breathing in and out the life of Christ, our souls come alive.

And when you think about it, isn't that what prayer is? It's breathing. You wake up and breathe in grace. You read a verse and ask God how to live it out. You drive to work and share with him what's on your heart. You walk out of a difficult meeting and release to him the pain you carry. When you laugh or wrestle with your kids, stand transfixed by a sunset, walk hand in hand with your spouse, relish a meal with friends, get lost in conversation, or hear a song that causes your heart to swell—prayer is the whisper: *Thank you.* Prayer is a dynamic reciprocity. Prayer is awareness that all of life is a gift.

It's interesting how prayer makes you aware of both how good God is and how petty some of your issues actually are. Not that they don't matter, but somehow, as you stand on the mountain with God, their magnitude seems to shrink. Maybe it's because God is eternal, and the scope of his being outweighs the anxiety we carry. In a sense, prayer lifts you out of time and connects you to the One who transcends it. It unites you to the One who sees the narrative arc of your life—who stands outside and yet is intimately within the story he has written for you.

Prayer frees you from the pressing urgency of the now—while simultaneously grounding you in the reality of I Am. The novelist Thomas Pynchon introduced an intriguing concept in his book *Gravity's Rainbow* that I think can be applied to prayer: He wrote, "Personal density . . . is directly proportional to temporal bandwidth."[4] Your "temporary bandwidth" represents your awareness of the past and future. In other words, the more you understand yourself through the infinite eyes of the God who made you, the more grounded and centered you become. Prayer gives your soul a sense of gravitas, a sacred immensity that moors you in every season. So instead of being

blown gossamer-like through life—easily influenced and swayed—
you possess a personal density.

Add to your faith goodness.

The only question is: Will we wait on him long enough to anchor
us with his "weight of glory" (2 Corinthians 4:17 ESV)?

CHOOSING STILLNESS

A number of years ago, a *Washington Post* journalist conducted an
experiment. He asked Joshua Bell, one of the world's most prodigiously
talented violinists, if he would perform at a DC subway station. Keep
in mind, Joshua is used to packed-out crowds, concert halls, and tele-
vision audiences. Had he lived in ancient Greece, they would have said
he possessed *arete*. But on this day, he was to impersonate a busker: a
stray musician scrounging up a few coins to pay for lunch. He walked
down into the subway, cradling his multimillion-dollar sixteenth-
century handcrafted Stradivarius violin, leaned against a wall, and
began to play. The exquisitely executed songs reverberated throughout
the station halls. Over a thousand people stampeded by, tapping on
their phones, talking to friends, heading to work, too preoccupied to
even notice. Only a handful of people stopped to listen, including a
woman who instantly recognized Bell because she had just seen him
play the night before at the Library of Congress. She couldn't believe
he was there. She handed him twenty dollars.[5]

It's a fascinating experiment; and for me, deeply convicting. I don't
even want to know how many days I've spent hustling through life like
that busy subway crowd. Distracted, blown weightless as I live out of
striving. Meanwhile, from some distant corner in my crowded soul,
God calls out to me. *Be still and know that I am God.*

Blaise Pascal once said, "Man's unhappiness springs from one thing alone, his incapacity to stay quietly in one room."[6] Ouch. But for me, it's worse. There are times I can't even stay quiet in my own mind. Can you relate? Even when I try to slow down and focus on the goodness of God, my confetti-like thoughts put up a fight. I'm so used to the noise, the stimuli, the meetings, the endless access to texts, email, social media, and Netflix, that pausing for prayer feels like torture.

Researchers from Microsoft found in 2015 that the average American's attention span had dropped to eight seconds.[7] That's right. If you happen to get to the end of this page, you're *way* ahead of the curve. What's even more depressing is that some fish have an attention span of nine seconds. We make Dory from *Finding Nemo* look like a genius.

Our squandered ability to be present and thoughtfully reflect is undeniably contributing to our inner sense of disorientation. Our soul needs a center, a source of gravity, if it's to flourish. So God patiently implores us to renounce our golden calves, climb back up the mountain, sit in his presence, and allow his unhurried Spirit to reawaken what's been numbed by distraction. As Tim Keller explains:

> Prayer is the only entryway into genuine self-knowledge. It is also the main way we experience deep change—the reordering of our loves. Prayer is how God gives us so many of the unimaginable things he has for us. Indeed, prayer makes it safe for God to give us many of the things we most desire. It is the way we know God, the way we finally treat God *as* God. Prayer is simply the key to everything we need to do and be in life. We must learn to pray. We have to.[8]

How do we pray like this? Let's see what Jesus had to say.

SIXTY-SIX SIMPLE WORDS

In Luke's gospel, the disciples came to Jesus with a pressing question: "Lord, teach us to pray" (11:1). They didn't say "teach us how to be successful" or "teach us how to build a bigger platform." They asked about prayer because they had seen how it was everything to Jesus. He slipped away in the early morning hours, retreated to quiet places, and poured out his heart to his Father. He would then return with unrushed clarity and authority; demons fled, raging storms subsided, and the sick were healed. For Jesus, prayer was the spark that ignited revolution, and the disciples wanted in on it.

Jesus answered their question, not with a stack of philosophical books but with these sixty-six heartfelt words found in Matthew 6, now known as the Lord's Prayer. Let's soak in some of them:

> Our Father in heaven,
> Hallowed be Your name.
> Your kingdom come.
> Your will be done
> On earth as it is in heaven.
> Give us this day our daily bread.
> And forgive us our debts,
> As we forgive our debtors.
> And do not lead us into temptation,
> But deliver us from the evil one.
> For Yours is the kingdom and the power and the glory
> forever. Amen. (vv. 9–13 NKJV)

I love how straightforward and unpretentious Jesus' words are. Prayer doesn't have to be a long, convoluted dissertation or eloquent sermon. It's just the real you delighting in the real God.

A few years ago, I heard a story about a dad who was trying to teach his four-year-old daughter how to pray. He kissed her goodnight, stepped out of the room, and pressed his ear against the door expecting to hear a prayer. Instead, he heard her singing the ABC song with gusto. He stepped back in. "Sweetie, I thought I asked you to pray?" She said, "I'm trying, Daddy, but it's so hard. I figured if I just sang the alphabet, Jesus could put all the letters together!"

That story reminds me of the quote: "It is better in prayer to have a heart without words than words without a heart."[9] As Paul reassured us, even if all we can do is groan in prayer (or recite the alphabet), God hears us anyway (Romans 8:26).

> SOMETIMES THE MOST BEAUTIFUL PRAYERS ARE NOT WORDS AT ALL, BUT THE FRAGILE PIECES OF YOU JUST SHOWING UP.

Sometimes the most beautiful prayers are not words at all, but the fragile pieces of you just showing up.

Our Father

For many people, *father* is a loaded word. They may see it as gendered terminology, or part of an oppressive, sexist, outdated view of the world. Others associate it with toxic masculinity or the patriarchy. Still others think of their own absent father, which often evokes memories of fear or a dysfunctional upbringing.

I know people who really struggle with calling God *Father*. Some don't do it at all. One denomination, to avoid offending people, just did away with the word altogether. They replaced *Father, Son,* and *Spirit* with "Rainbow of Promise, Ark of Salvation, Dove of Peace."[10]

Here's the problem with that approach. Eliminating language doesn't eliminate our soul's desire for a loving father. Although we may wish to safeguard our hearts, refusing to call God *Father* could actually prevent us from healing. Why? Because he is a *good* Father. He is strong, gracious, patient, and astonishingly kind. Though we are flawed, he loves us perfectly. And he wants to restore what's been damaged and broken in our past—and maybe even in our present too—by showing us what a true Father looks like.

Father was, by far, the most common word Jesus used in his relationship with God. But when he said it, it wasn't in a cold "Luke, I am your father" kind of way. He used the Aramaic word *Abba*, which is closer to our words *daddy* or *papa*. Abba is intimacy and friendship. Like the times I came home from work when my daughter, Amelia, was young, and she'd fly down the stairs into my arms: "Daddy!" Abba is you holding your son for the very first time or walking teary-eyed with your daughter down the aisle. Abba is closeness, tenderness, and boundless love.

When Jesus began his prayer with *Abba*, it was a revolutionary approach to God. Other religious systems never envisioned God as Abba. Think of Baal, Ra, Dagon, or Zeus. They were distant, emotionally aloof gods. Sure, you prayed to them, but the emphasis wasn't on love but obligation: You sacrificed the goat, and the gods sent rain. You gave wheat, and the gods gave you an Apple Watch. It was all very contractual.

The way Jesus related to his Father, however, wasn't through contract but love.

The cynical part of me thinks, *Well, obviously Jesus called him Father. He's part of the Trinity, isn't he? He's God. I'd say their relationship was pretty tight.* True. But here's the amazing thing: The Bible teaches the same relationship Jesus had with the Father is the relationship you can enjoy as well.

Let's go back to Paul's words in Romans 8:15: "The Spirit you received brought about your adoption to sonship. And by him we cry, 'Abba, Father.'" Just like when a child is born, and a loving father's heart fuses onto that child from day one, God's heart is enduringly bound to you. And even though parenting is messy—to paraphrase Jerry Seinfeld, it sometimes feels like having a blender without a lid[11]—God is tirelessly devoted to your flourishing.

There will always be people in your life who will bad-mouth you, judge you, or abandon you. But God is not like anyone else. He is a father whose love encompasses you completely. And unconditionally. You've been adopted as his beloved.

In the first century, infanticide was much more common than adoption. If a child had disabilities or was the wrong gender, or if the parents just didn't want it, they would leave it outside to die. There are historical records of people discarding their infants on the side of mountains or throwing them onto piles of trash. There was, however, one group of people who wasn't okay with that: Christians. They climbed the mountains to rescue the infants, adopt them, and take them home.[12]

Do you realize how God has done the same for you?

You may have been hurt by friends, family, or the church. You may have been rejected by someone you trusted. You may carry trauma from your past that makes it hard to believe in a good Father, let alone pray. You can't imagine climbing a mountain, like Moses did, just to be with God.

I want you to know that's okay. Even if you can barely groan, he is still your Abba. Even if you can hardly stand, he runs to you and robes you in kindness. Even if you can scarcely take another step, he climbs the mountain and holds you close in his arms. God has eternally loved you, which means you don't pray to be accepted; you pray *because you already are.*

BREATHE IN

Since prayer is how God's goodness flows into us, enlarging our souls to come alive, let's be sure we understand *how*. You can start now by accepting that you're implicitly loved and adored by him.

Take a deep breath. Close your eyes. Call him Abba.

Go ahead. Ask him to speak to you.

But I hear nothing.

Don't worry. Sometimes prayer isn't about you hearing from God at all. It's about God hearing you. It's opening your heart to all that's wounded inside, exposing the lies you've been living, the secrets you've been hiding, the grief you've been suppressing. Prayer is the moment you stop running and allow his goodness—which has been with you all along—to quicken your winded soul. As theologian J.C. Ryle revealed, "Prayer is to faith what breath is to life."[13]

In Hebrew, the word *soul* is *nephesh*. What's interesting is that *nephesh* comes from another word, *naphash*, which means "to take a deep breath." It's like a sharp inhale followed by a grateful exhale when you narrowly avoid an accident on a freeway or hear news that someone you love is okay. You feel nothing but release and relief. You can breathe again.

Through prayer, your soul gasps, "I'm here. I made it. It's been a stressful day, or a hard week; but in your presence, Lord, I can breathe again." Like Adam, whose soul came alive through the breath of God, prayer is proximity. Prayer is the whisper: "I'm home."

As I shared in chapter 1, my wife, Elyssa, had a medical emergency before I wrote this book. She had been sick for several weeks, but then over the course of a couple days, her breathing grew heavy, and her health deteriorated. I drove her to the doctor, and immediately after they took a scan of her chest, they put her in an ambulance. Her right lung was 75 percent collapsed. The medical term is *spontaneous pneumothorax*. I came to learn that basically means: "Your lung collapsed, and we have no idea why." It's super rare and extremely dangerous.

For over two weeks she was in the hospital, undergoing surgeries, seeing specialists, and fighting acute pain. At one point, they gave her a little plastic tube with a clear box attached to it. "Breathe into this," they said, "and it will help us monitor your oxygen levels. Plus, the deeper you breathe, the more you can heal." It hurt like crazy, but because she's way braver than I, she did it several times a day until she came home.

Think about those words: *The deeper you breathe, the more you can heal.*

That's what your soul is longing for right now.

To heal.

To rest.

To recover.

To belong.

To know God's goodness.

And that's what your Father offers. We only need to breathe in.

Come Alive

Waiting on God is a soul-forming art. It's learning to be okay with silence and releasing the tiresome need to know and have all the answers. It's choosing contentment over certainty. Waiting is the space between your fear and God's peace. Spend some time waiting on God now. You may want to go for a walk. Or find a place where you can put away distractions and be still. Take a deep breath. Open your heart to God's healing presence.

As you silently remain in his presence, is there anything that he's bringing to the surface of your life? Listen to what the Holy Spirit might be saying. What is he stirring inside you? Are there any fears you need to acknowledge? Sins you need to confess? Hopes you need to name?

Remind yourself of who you are: his son or daughter, and that you are fiercely and unconditionally loved by him. Take time to thank and worship him for the love he's shown to you. Name the places where you've seen his goodness in your life.

5.

LIVE WITHOUT WALLS

Add to your faith . . . knowledge.

—2 PETER 1:5

A child's first words are always a thrilling moment for any family. Usually the first word is *mama* or *dada*. Or maybe *dog*.

My daughter's first word was *iPod*.

Seriously. She had just turned one, and *already* she was addicted to technology. One of my favorite pictures shows her standing confidently in our living room with a black iPod Classic (remember those?) clipped onto the side of the diaper she was wearing, along with a pair of colossal headphones bulging over her ears. Her expression was priceless: brows furrowed, eyes locked in and serious, lips looking like they desperately wanted to sing along. My wife swears the picture will make for amazing blackmail someday.

Fifteen years later, she's joined the rest of us with her new favorite word: *iPhone*.

Did you know Americans spend more than four hours every day looking at their phones?[1] Half of that time is browsing social media, and almost an hour is texting. We pick up our phones sixty-three times a day. We tap, swipe, and click a staggering 2,617 times a day.[2] There's something about the lure of limitless information that our brains can't resist; but, as it turns out, our souls can't contain what we take in.

They say knowledge is power. Is it though?

According to the cognitive psychologist Daniel Levitin, all this knowledge comes with a cost because the brain has limits on how much information it can consume. "The processing capacity of the conscious mind has been estimated at 120 bits per second," he wrote.[3] For reference, when you have a conversation with someone, it takes up about 60 bits. That means, at most, you can talk to two people at once before experiencing neural overload—that is, unless you're an introvert, in which case it's more like half a conversation! As a result, every online meeting you participate in, every tweet or message, and every comment or like on TikTok is contending for limited resources in your brain. Maybe that's why so many of us have what's called Zoom fatigue: a form of mental burnout resulting in concentration difficulties, forgetfulness, frustration, and irritability.[4] Our brains are buried by information, and our lives are struggling to catch up; meanwhile, what we are taking in is not always beneficial. In BJ Fogg's research on habit formation, he discovered what he calls the Information-Action Fallacy:

> Information alone does not reliably change behavior. This is a common mistake people make, even well-meaning professionals. The assumption is this: If we give people the right information, it will change their attitudes, which in turn will change their behaviors.[5]

Maybe what matters most, then, is not simply acquiring knowledge, but rather the kind and quality of that knowledge. Even more important is what we do with the knowledge we gain.

ROOTED IN LOVE

The second gift Peter invited us to add to our faith is "knowledge." But as you've probably guessed, he used a word that meant so much more than acquiring information. In his day it meant "to receive, grasp, and participate." Peter was talking about a kind of knowledge that looks more like wisdom—awareness that leads to action.

When I was in college, one of my roommates decided his New Year's resolution was to gain more muscle. He went to the local GNC and picked up a massive barrel of protein powder with the picture of a ripped bodybuilder embellishing the packaging. Every day, multiple times a day, he would guzzle the stuff. Funny thing was, he rarely worked out! Four months later he had gained a lot of weight, but it was the wrong kind. Turns out, protein powder alone won't make you look like Thor. And knowledge alone won't make your soul flourish—unless you're willing to put in the time.

C. S. Lewis adroitly noted the difference between *intellectual ascent* and *relational trust*. He knew many scholars who were extremely intelligent, but what they lacked was an authentic, flourishing relationship with God. In his book *The Great Divorce*, which describes an allegorical bus tour of hell, the narrator meets a highly sophisticated theologian and invites him to get on board and journey with him to heaven. The theologian refuses, citing a compulsory meeting at a theological society where he is slated to speak.[6] *They have theological societies in hell?*

Having been a part of a few, I'm not surprised! Just kidding. But Lewis was making a powerful point: If all our learning isn't leading us closer to God, then it has only qualified us to become really smart demons. As Paul declared in 1 Corinthians 13:2, "If I have the gift of prophecy and can fathom all mysteries and all knowledge, and if I have a faith that can move mountains, but do not have love, I am nothing."

Knowledge must be rooted in love.

This explains why *goodness* precedes knowledge on Peter's road map to flourishing. We begin with intimacy: our lives rooted in God, investing time in prayer, sitting at his feet. And from that posture we learn not only who he is, but also who *we are*. Learning is the outgrowth of coming to him.

What does this mean practically? How can we add to our faith knowledge?

Let's focus on two different kinds of knowings: the knowledge God gives us in his Word and the knowledge he reveals to us about ourselves.

KNOWING GOD'S WORD

As followers of Jesus, our primary source of spiritual knowing is Scripture:

- Proverbs 2:6 reads, "For the LORD gives wisdom; from his mouth come knowledge and understanding."
- Second Timothy 2:7 says we should pay careful attention to God's Word, and he will "give [us] understanding in everything" (ESV).
- Isaiah 55:10–11 gives us this promise: "As the rain and the snow come down from heaven, and do not return to it without

watering the earth and making it bud and flourish . . . so is my word that goes out from my mouth."

The Isaiah verses offer such a pristine visual promise. God says even as water causes the earth to flourish, so, too, does his Word create flourishing in our souls. Why is that? One important reason is, like prayer, God's Word anchors us to a larger story. It reminds us of all the dynamic ways he has been working throughout history and accomplishing his mission—and how someday all of creation will be redeemed and restored.

I don't know about you, but it is so easy for me to lose the plot and instead become hyperfocused on whatever drama is clawing for my attention. Psychologists call this the *availability heuristic*—our tendency to be influenced by the tyranny of urgent things rather than the peace that comes from seeing life holistically.

A good example of this happened when news first broke about COVID-19. Like dominoes, news stories dropped one after another: An NBA team walked off the court. Tom Hanks announced that he and his wife had tested positive. Disneyland shut its gates. Then everyone, seemingly in unison, made a mad rush to their local grocery store to line up for . . . toilet paper.

Toilet paper? Why, of all things, did it cause us to panic? Why not, you know, food? Personally, I think someone could do a fascinating dissertation on the Freudian psychology of that. But one explanation is *availability heuristic*. We didn't know what was happening, and our limited experience of disasters had taught us toilet paper was generally the first to go.

Clearly, something we all struggle with, especially in disruptive times, is perspective.

We see this even in the history of the word *disaster*, which derives from the Latin words *dis*, meaning "without," and *astro*, which means "star." A disaster is thus living "without a star." In antiquity, stars kept travelers and sailors moving on course—so to do without them would have been catastrophic. How about us? Where do we go when the night is dark and our souls are struggling to find true north?

Scripture faithfully reminds us that no matter what we're facing—storms, trials, difficult situations, difficult people, pandemics—God's purposes are still being accomplished. He's our guiding star, the bedrock that grounds our tousled hearts. When everything around us is shaking, the Bible shouts: He is an unshakable God. He's got this.

The Jewish people understood the need to orient their souls around this truth, and it's why seven times a year they gathered with friends and family to have festivals. For days they hit the pause button—ate, danced, read Scripture, and reminded each other of all the amazing things God had done for their ancestors. In the Bible, this was actually a command. That's right: God commanded his people to have parties! In Deuteronomy, God urged parents to be faithful in reminding their children about the larger story they were a part of: "Fix these words of mine in your hearts and minds; tie them as symbols on your hands and bind them on your foreheads. Teach them to your children, talking about them when you sit at home and when you walk along the road, when you lie down and when you get up" (11:18–19).

This awareness of God's faithfulness produced a collective and even generational *shalom*: a calm centeredness and ability to trust God in the face of whatever dire situations stood before them. Because that's what stories do. Especially the true ones. As Bill Buford, a former editor at the *New Yorker*, argued:

> Stories . . . protect us from chaos . . . Implicit in the extraordinary revival of storytelling is the possibility that we need stories—that they are a fundamental unit of knowledge, the foundation of

memory, essential to the way we make sense . . . of our personal and collective trajectories.[7]

Every time you immerse yourself in the Bible, you're fortifying your soul from the chaos that conspires to leave you disoriented. You're buttressing your inner self with knowledge of God's *withness* in your life; his commitment to your flourishing, and the flourishing of all creation. The verses, prophecies, poetry, parables, letters, history—even the hard-to-understand tales of colorful characters and the monotonous lists of names—they're all there to remind you of God's encompassing presence with humanity. The Bible is the oldest story; of love lost and love found. And clasping all the pages together, a Narrator who never gives up on the world he created. That knowledge alone will cause your soul to burst into life. You'll thrive in the awareness that God is with you and has called you to participate in his mission for the world. You'll know the truth, and the truth will set you free.

> THE BIBLE IS THE OLDEST STORY; OF LOVE LOST AND LOVE FOUND. AND CLASPING ALL THE PAGES TOGETHER, A NARRATOR WHO NEVER GIVES UP ON THE WORLD HE CREATED.

OPENING GOD'S WORD

What, then, are some good practices for reading Scripture? I would recommend beginning with prayer. Again, this takes us back to *adding to our faith goodness.* Before we open the Bible, we first need to invite the Lord to speak to us. Approach his Word with a humble, teachable heart, not forcing our own agenda on it. This is especially relevant when you think of all the manipulative ways the Bible has been used historically. With it, people have justified slavery, war, colonialism, and the oppression of women. You can quote chapters and verses to get away with virtually anything. Case in point: Frank Sinatra is rumored to have said, "Alcohol may be man's worst enemy, but the Bible says love your enemy!"[8]

That's what I like to call the "inkblot way" of reading the Bible. You may remember inkblots from Psychology 101. Someone shows you a mess of ink on a page, and what you see supposedly reveals your hidden thoughts and desires. When we project on the Bible what we want it to say, instead of accepting what it's truly saying, we're not only missing the point—we're forfeiting an opportunity to grow. But when you pray, especially if it's done in community, it gives your heart an opportunity to synchronize with the heart of God; it shatters your resistance, biases, and distorted perspective and puts you in a posture of unassumed listening and learning.

Another helpful practice when reading Scripture is to commit to reading it in its entirety, from Genesis to Revelation, because the Bible is a story—and like any story, it has a beginning, middle, and end. As you read it, the drama builds, the characters develop, and the threads connect. When you see the Bible as an unfolding narrative, it gives you an appreciation and sense of place and protects you from the very real temptation to cherry-pick.

The Bible isn't meant to be dissected like a specimen in a lab. It's meant to be gazed at like a piece of art. The Bible isn't a formula; it's a story. And a messy one at that. Spend time reading it, and you'll quickly discover (usually by the second or third page!) that it's awkward, wild, messy, and volatile. It will defy your sense of logic, contradict your cultural values, and challenge your prejudice. But that's all part of its beauty. The Bible wasn't written so you could master it, but so it could master you. It's a drama that wants to sweep you off your feet with its tension, tragedy, and mystery. Let its words sit with you, challenge you, and heal you. Because, as Paul promised, it will: "Every part of Scripture is God-breathed and useful one way or another—showing us truth, exposing our rebellion, correcting our mistakes, training us to live God's way. Through the Word we are put together and shaped up for the tasks God has for us" (2 Timothy 3:16–17 MSG).

KNOWING YOURSELF

Now let's discuss the knowledge God wants to reveal to you about yourself. As you draw close to him, spending time in prayer and Scripture, questions about the welfare of your soul will naturally arise: *Am I doing what God has told me to do? Am I thriving spiritually, mentally, emotionally, and physically? Or am I struggling? Are there wounds in my life that need healing? Am I hiding issues that are unresolved or actively preventing my flourishing? Is God inviting me to something new: a job, dream, or place? Am I living out of my true self? Or projecting a false self—a version of me that betrays my calling?*

A prayer I often hear in church circles is, "God, would you reveal yourself to us?" I understand the request, but I'm learning that spiritual growth isn't just about God revealing himself to us; we need him to reveal *us* to *ourselves*. I think of David's plea in Psalm 19:12: "Forgive my hidden faults." Or Augustine's prayer:

> Lord Jesus, let me know myself and know You. . . .
> Look upon me, that I may love You.
> Call me that I may see you, and for ever enjoy You.[9]

Some people bristle at prayers like that. Aren't we supposed to deny ourselves? Didn't Jesus say we must lose our lives to find them? Absolutely. But it's hard to lose something you've never found. Sometimes our perspective is so clouded by distraction, busyness, trauma, shame, or sin that we can't even see into our own souls. If you aren't in tune with your true self, then how can you ever authentically relate to God? Unity with God—or with others, for that matter—is impossible if you're divided within yourself. Thus, a vital step to any healthy relationship is first understanding and owning your story.

Authenticity is the seedbed of belonging.

FINDING WHO YOU WERE MADE TO BE

Psalm 51:10 is not a long prayer, but it takes a lifetime to learn: "Create in me a pure heart, O God, and renew a steadfast spirit within me." I always assumed "pure" meant the opposite of sin. Yet David, whose life was imploding from scandal and failure when he wrote it, wasn't simply acknowledging his brokenness; he was crying out for wholeness. A pure heart—that is, a holy or whole heart—is a heart undiluted by pretense. It's an unmasked, what-you-see-is-what-you-get transparency. David was torn up over the years he had tried to fake it before God and others.

"Create in me a pure heart" is the anguish of a man who was weary of the falseness in his soul. As knowledge of himself grew, so did his desire to renounce deception and be who the Spirit had first called him to be: a man after God's own heart (1 Samuel 13:14). There were moments, especially early on, when he beheld this vision. But something happened over the years. Perhaps it was discouragement, boredom, loneliness, or frustration as a leader, but in time he built up protective walls that obstructed his capacity to flourish.

God wanted to tear the walls down. *Adding to your faith knowledge* means we must be willing to let God do the same in us—allow him to identify and dismantle the barriers in our soul that hold us back from the story we were made for.

Like David's, the inauthentic walls we develop as adults often emerge because of disappointment, disillusionment, or sometimes unhealthy experiences in our childhood or adolescence. Think about a newborn. There's free-flowing synergy between their true self and lived self. If they're hungry, they let the world know, right? If they're happy, you can't keep them from giggling. Kids are open books. They don't fake it.

As they get older—maybe because of a trauma, peer pressure, social factors, family dynamics, the jobs they take on, or expectations people put on them—they put up walls to shield their hearts. They also project images of what others expect them to be and develop coping mechanisms to deal with heartache.

In my childhood a way I dealt with the upheaval I witnessed at home was to withdraw. I still remember as a middle schooler going for long walks alone in a field near our house just to try to figure things out. Those who study interpersonal conflict and how humans respond to it suggest that some people are skunks and others are turtles. The skunks make a stink and let everyone know how they feel. Turtles clam up in their shells and shut the world out. Which one are you? I was the turtle. Even now, there are moments when I find it hard to express emotion if I'm hurt, exhausted, or discouraged. It's so much easier to shut down.

But here's the painful reality in our quest to know ourselves: The more we hide fragments of our true selves, the more broken we become. As Saint Teresa of Avila observed: "Almost all problems in the spiritual life stem from a lack of self-knowledge."[10] In time, a gap emerges between our *souls* and *roles*. We act one way in front of our friends, family, fellow students, or coworkers; meanwhile, something inside us is screaming, *This isn't who I am.* Author, activist, and educator Parker J. Palmer was exploring this gap when he wrote:

> I yearn to be whole, but dividedness often seems the easier choice. A "still, small voice" speaks the truth about me, my work, or the world. I hear it and yet act as if I did not. I withhold a personal gift that might serve a good end or commit myself to a project that I do not really believe in. I keep silent on an issue I should address or actively break faith with one of my own convictions. . . . A fault line runs down the middle of my life, and whenever it cracks open—divorcing my words and actions from the truth I hold within—things around me get shaky and start to fall apart.[11]

Every soul yearns to be whole. There's a Hasidic tale of a rabbi named Zusya who reflected on this as an old man. He said, "In the coming world, they will not ask me: 'Why were you not Moses?' They will ask me, 'Why were you not Zusya?'"[12] Maturity is learning to grow in the realization that God's utmost desire for you is not that you'd try and fulfill someone else's dream for your life but that you'd be true to his dream for you.

Understanding that can take years of prayer, faithful and honest friends, wrestling, acknowledging, mentoring, and counseling. Walls take years to develop and can take many more to come down. But as you add to your faith knowledge, the more you'll become increasingly aware of the barriers in your life that are keeping your soul from flourishing. You'll have a growing ache to be, in David's words, *pure.* You'll become more fully yourself, alive and free.

LIVING WHO YOU WERE MADE TO BE

Kierkegaard, the Danish philosopher, revealed that the Danish word for freedom is *friheden*. It comes from the root word *fri*, which means "proposal." If you're married, recall the moment when you got on one knee to propose to the love of your life. Or when someone asked you and you said "yes." That simple word binds you to that person, doesn't it? And because not everyone understands love's reasons, it can be difficult to explain the immensity of your commitment. A friend once told me: "Dominic, the wedding ring is the world's smallest handcuff." I laughed at his cynicism, and then I realized why he was still single.

To those on the outside, love may look like bondage. But to those on the inside, it's freedom.

As you learn to live without walls, spending time cultivating your relationship with God, loving him, discovering the contours of his heart, you'll find yourself, in strange and beautiful ways, both constrained and free. Constrained because the way of Jesus always summons us beyond the urges of our fallen self. Liberated because in his presence you can be most fully your redeemed self. Since God offers you boundless acceptance, you don't have to pretend to be someone you're not. The walls of performance, shame, sin, confusion about your identity, what others have said to you or about you—all gradually acquiesce to belonging. As twentieth-century existentialist Albert Camus wrote: "In order to be, never try to seem."[13] Sometimes the only way to find yourself is by letting go of what you've been striving to become.

SOMETIMES THE ONLY WAY TO FIND YOURSELF IS BY LETTING GO OF WHAT YOU'VE BEEN STRIVING TO BECOME.

I think back to another moment in David's life, this time when he faced the nine-foot-tall Goliath in battle. King Saul didn't have the guts to face Goliath himself, so he offered David his armor: "Here, take my shield. Here's my helmet. Use my sword." David tried to put them on and quickly realized it was super awkward and clunky. Saul was taller than he was and had years of experience wearing armor. Besides, David had never fought a giant. He was a shepherd with a slingshot, not a warrior with a heavy sword. He took the armor off and, with a single rock, took down the lumbering Philistine (1 Samuel 17).

When you try to wear someone else's armor, it's exhausting. Maybe you've tried. I know I have. It could be your position at work. You joined the company because of family pressure, or someone you admired was incredibly successful there and you want to be like them. So you give it a shot. But the longer you're there, you can't shake the nagging suspicion that something is wrong. Your joy is gone. Your creativity is being suppressed. The *shalom* that once carried you is replaced by a heavy burden of unhealthy expectations and pressures. If you stop long enough, you may realize no amount of money is worth the price you're paying.

The wrong armor could be a dating relationship. Everyone thought you'd be perfect together, and you did too . . . until you weren't. Months in, you still know it's not right; but it's tough to muster the courage to let go and move on.

Or think about how we curate our lives on social media. A while ago I saw a story about a woman who dreamed of becoming an influencer. She moved to New York, then spent all of her money on designer handbags and shopping sprees. She incessantly posted VSCO-girl pictures of her lifestyle. It got her thirteen thousand followers but left her depressed and ten thousand dollars in debt. When interviewed, she opened up about all the pressure she felt to fit a certain mold, how she wanted to live a *Sex and the City* fantasy, and how she mimicked all the other celebrities she followed online. But then she realized it was all a game. She gave up her striving and eventually paid off her debt.[14]

Freedom is coming to a point when you realize the armor you're wearing doesn't fit anymore. It's when you're sick of pretending, tired of conforming and compromising who you really are just to pacify others. Freedom is breathing deeply and saying: "This is who God created me to be." Maybe people around you won't understand. Maybe it will mean a cut in pay. Or a season of singleness. Maybe it will mean saying no a time or two or a little less security because you do. But what you'll get in return is *integrity*. Integrity is related to the word we considered earlier: *integrate*, or to make whole. That's God's dream for you— wholeness as you live out your calling. The greatest gift you could give the world is the story God has given you.

THE GREATEST GIFT YOU COULD GIVE THE WORLD IS THE STORY GOD HAS GIVEN YOU.

David was most fully himself when he set the armor down and seized what God had given him all along: a slingshot. It didn't seem like much. I'm sure people around him scoffed. But he stepped forward anyway—armor-less, free, and full of faith.

He realized it's far better to die in the freedom of authenticity than to merely exist under the weight of deception.

What has God given you? What's in your hand? When you listen to your life, *truly* listen, what are the longings your heart is begging you to hear? What are your interests? Dreams? Desires? What are you good at? What makes you laugh? What fills you with joy? What are the gifts God has entrusted to you?

Like David, it probably won't *feel* like enough. It rarely does. The greatest lie the enemy wants you to believe is that what God has given you isn't enough. Satan loves to shame you for who you are, where you came from, what you don't have, how you look, the color of your skin, your intellect, your education, your background, or the mistakes of your past. He wants you to retreat from your calling instead of boldly stepping into it. He wants to kill your joy through comparison. He wants you perpetually stuck in your habits, trapped in the familiar cycle of sin, unable to break free. He wants to discourage you, whispering in your ear how far you have to go and how hard the road will be to get there.

And, sure, it *is* hard.

It's hard coming face-to-face with our past, our failures, our guilt, and all the ways we've lived a divided life. It's hard to acknowledge we've spent years fighting the wrong battles or fixating on the wrong goals. It's hard to make necessary changes or to set the armor down. It's hard to live without walls.

But it's also the only way your soul can flourish. It's the only way to be free.

And in more ways than you may dare to know, the irrefutable truth is that you already *are* free: "Where the Spirit of the Lord is, there is freedom" (2 Corinthians 3:17).

The more you add to your faith knowledge, both knowledge of God's Word and yourself, you'll discover you are free to change. You are free to choose. You are free to adapt, evolve, and grow. The forces, ideologies, regrets, fears, choices, and heartaches that once defined your life don't have to shape your life anymore. The labels others use about you are wrong because this moment, and every moment to come, is a blank slate, an unwritten script, a story with hope as the ending. "You, my brothers and sisters, were called to be free" (Galatians 5:13).

And as the poet Emily Dickinson stirringly conveyed, we "dwell in Possibility."[15]

Your unfolding story is more than the boxes they put you in. You're changing. They may define and confine you because it fits a narrative, but God has liberated you. You're more than a note; you're an evolving symphony.

Embrace God's "new" for your life.

Come Alive

If you have a Bible nearby, pick it up and turn to Psalm 119:105. Before reading, take a moment to pray and ask the Lord to speak to you through his Word. Now read verse 105. How is God's Word a lamp for your feet and a light for your path? How does knowledge of God's Word direct you? We discussed how Scripture reminds us of the larger story God is writing. How does that bring comfort and courage to your life?

Next, read Psalm 51:10. Make it your prayer.

The word *pure* means "undivided or whole." Are there any areas in your life where you've been living a divided life? Are there any walls you've developed or built, perhaps even from childhood, that have held you back from living true to who God envisions you to be? Is there a disconnect between your soul and your role? What action could you take to live without walls: at work, at home, in your relationship with God or others?

6.

CONFRONTING YOUR SHADOW SIDE

And to knowledge, self-control.

—2 PETER 1:6

Have you noticed when you go into a bookstore or browse your phone for podcasts, you'll find hundreds of resources about how to improve yourself—how to lose weight, be a better parent, or overcome addictions—but you'll never see any about how to be a jerk, an arrogant narcissist, bitter, proud, jealous, or greedy? Turns out we've already got that down, thanks to our shadow side—the part of the soul that harbors sinful and unhealthy desires.

Every good story has a hero and a villain. In the story of our lives, we're both. As Mark Twain keenly perceived, "Everyone is a moon, and has a dark side which he never shows to anybody."[1]

In book two of *The Republic*, a dialogue written by Plato in 375 BCE, the philosopher recounted the legend of a lowly shepherd named Gyges and his mysterious ring of invisibility.

One day as Gyges was watching over the king's sheep, a violent earthquake split the ground near where he was standing, causing a yawning chasm to appear. Peering carefully into the ruptured earth, Gyges was shocked to discover the skeletal remains of a giant, ancient corpse wearing a luminous golden ring. Carefully, he lowered himself beside the corpse, pulled the ring from its bony finger, and put it on his own.

A few nights later, as he huddled with other shepherds around a fire, a Gollum-esque Gyges began toying with his newfound ring, turning it this way and that. Suddenly, as he twisted the face of the ring toward the palm of his hand, he became instantly invisible to his friends, who began to act as if he were no longer there. He turned it again, then reappeared.

Gyges sat in wonder as the ring's potential dawned on him. He knew it was time to act.

In short order he arranged to become a messenger to the king, which would give him unfettered proximity to the throne. Then, with no fear of being caught, he activated the ring, utilizing its powers to seduce the king's wife. With her help, and a knife she supplied, Gyges snuck up to the sleeping king and assassinated him, stealing his kingdom.

This disturbing tale from Plato's pen illustrates how anyone, no matter how moral and pious they appear, would ultimately succumb to the allure of the ring. You see, the real problem isn't the ring; it's us. All the ring does is reveal what lies buried inside our hearts.

We all have a different person lurking beneath the carefully chiseled mask of who we think we are. And no one knew that better than the apostle Peter, who urged us to add self-control to our faith. He knew what it was like to be nearly swallowed up by his inner abyss. I'm sure not a day went by when he didn't regret what happened at the enemy's fire where he denounced his Rabbi, Jesus. He recalled how effortlessly he spit out the words: "I don't know the man!" (Matthew 26:72).

Later, Jesus warned him, "Simon, Simon, Satan has asked to sift all of you as wheat" (Luke 22:31). Those words should stop every one of us in our tracks. Because they're true of our lives too. God said a similar thing to Cain: "Sin is crouching at your door; it desires to have you, but you must rule over it" (Genesis 4:7).

But how do we "rule over" the sin that's disturbingly present in our shadow side?

How do we confront the thoughts, attitudes, and actions that conspire to ambush our flourishing?

And how do we step into a life of self-control?

NAMING THE SHADOWS

Defined, *self-control* means "master, conquest, or dominion." It's where we derive the phrase "get a grip"—what you'll hear if you're in the middle of a meltdown or if your emotions are getting the better of you. In the first century, it characterized someone who had mastered their passions: a boxer who restrained anger, a surgeon who tamed fear, an artist who overcame frustration. The idea is, since there are dark places in your life that want to "wage war against your soul" (1 Peter 2:11), you must be proactive and bring everything under the influence of the Holy Spirit.

This naturally flows out of what we unpacked in the last chapter: knowledge. As we lean into our relationship with God, learning from him and gaining knowledge about ourselves, we'll soon encounter shadows lurking in the hidden corners of our lives. Stepping into the light makes that inevitable. Seventeenth-century archbishop Francois Fénelon described how horrifying that can be: "As that light increases, we see ourselves to be worse than we thought. We are amazed at our former blindness as we see issuing forth from the depths of our heart a whole swarm of shameful feelings, like filthy reptiles crawling from a hidden cave. We never could have believed that we had harboured such things, and we stand aghast as we watch them gradually appear."[2]

Waging war against darkness means being willing to own up to our shadows and call them what they are: *sin.* Some of the earliest Christians in church history believed there were seven: greed, pride, gluttony, sloth, envy, wrath, and lust. What's interesting is, when you look closer, you'll see how each of these sins is a corrupted form of 2 Peter 1:5–7. Corrupted goodness is greed; corrupted knowledge is pride; corrupted self-control is gluttony; corrupted perseverance is sloth; corrupted godliness is envy; corrupted mutual affection is wrath; and corrupted love is lust.

7 Virtues	7 Deadly Sins
Goodness	Greed
Knowledge	Pride
Self-control	Gluttony
Perseverance	Sloth
Godliness	Envy
Mutual Affection	Wrath
Love	Lust

In the fifth century, the Latin poet Prudentius wrote a poem describing a battle between these seven deadly sins and the seven virtues. The provocative title, *Psychomachia*, which could be the name of an eighties metal band, is translated the *Battle of the Spirits* or *Soul War*.

Psychomachia sounds a lot like life. Every day is a soul war, between sin and flourishing, between who we are and who God is calling us to be.

Superficially, we define sin as breaking rules or doing things our parents, society, or faith community would consider wrong. That's partially true. But more accurately, sin isn't just the violation of an external standard; it's the violation of your soul's truest identity and desire.

Your soul was made to live transparently before God. Think of Adam and Eve in Eden. They were unclothed and unashamed. They had nothing to hide as they walked with God through the lush garden. Their lives were unclouded by deception toward God and each other. But when they sinned and attempted to cover it up, their true selves vanished like Gyges as they hid in the bushes.

God called out to them: "Where are you?" (Genesis 3:9). Not because he didn't know, but because their souls were no longer wide open to his presence. And that was the devastating consequence: They had cut themselves off from the Source of flourishing.

What is sin, then?

Sin is misplaced desire. We could even say it's not *enough* desire—because our ultimate desire isn't for sin, which never satisfies anyway, but for the goodness of God. Sin is a kind of vandalism of the soul: the deforming of our inner beauty, disintegration of its wholeness, and the disruption of *shalom*. Sin is a meager shadow compared to the abundance of the Spirit-filled life. But the real tragedy is that it not only keeps you from experiencing God's best but also causes you to forget who you really are: a new creation, forgiven, set free, clean,

WHEN WE SIN, WE'RE CUTTING OURSELVES OFF FROM OUR SOULS' BREATH.

adopted as sons and daughters, called to live in freedom.

God created your soul to flourish as you walk in intimacy with him. Anything less than that, and anything we pursue in place of that, is selling out our God-given purpose. When we sin, we're cutting ourselves off from our souls' breath. Yet how many times do we suffocate our souls in hollow pursuits, chasing after things that leave us gasping for air?

KNOWING YOUR SHADOWS

Here's an interesting thought experiment. If you knew you could get away with literally anything with total anonymity and zero consequences, what would you do? If you had access to the same ring Gyges had, how would you spend your weekend? Where would you go? How would you use your power?

It's pretty scary how easily we'll forsake the flourishing life for the poverty of sin. And what's more sobering is the awareness that everyone is that way. Everyone you know struggles with primal desires, twisted motivations, repressed anger, bitterness, lust, hypocrisy, pride, and self-centeredness. Even the people you assume are mature and godly may surprise you by what they'd do with a golden ring.

Paul wrote about this with candor in Romans 7: "I do not understand what I do. For what I want to do I do not do, but what I hate I do . . . I have the desire to do what is good, but I cannot carry it out . . . What a wretched man I am!" (vv. 15, 18, 24).

Keep in mind, this confession was written after Paul had been walking with Jesus for twenty-five years. You'd think by then he'd have figured things out. But, instead, he identified within himself a battle that raged between light and shadow. *I do not understand what I do.* If you've ever tried a diet plan, you know exactly what Paul is talking about: the spirit is willing, but the ice cream is sweet!

Another interesting aspect of Paul's journey is that the more in faith he grew, the more heated the war inside him became. You can see this in a few of his autobiographical statements:

- At the onset of his ministry, a young Paul wrote: "I am the least of the apostles" (1 Corinthians 15:9).
- When he was middle-aged, he confessed, "I am less than the least of all the Lord's people" (Ephesians 3:8).
- At the end of his life, he announced: "I was the worst sinner of all!" (1 Timothy 1:15 CEV).

There seemed to be a progression in his life; the older he got, the more he recognized, and was repulsed by, the sinister presence of his shadow side.

Perhaps that's what maturity really looks like: not pretending to be strong and invulnerable but admitting our aching need for grace.

Years ago when my wife and I lived in Vienna, we studied German at a university. She's always had a thing for languages and is brilliant at it. Not so with me, but I did learn a word that stuck: *doppelgänger*. It means "double walker." In mythology, a doppelgänger is basically your creepy, nefarious twin—a ghostly phantom that resembles you but acts in ways you never normally would. It's Paul's "wretched man."

Have you ever done something, said something, or made a

decision that made you sick to your stomach when you woke up the next morning? *How could I . . . ?* Welcome to your doppelgänger. Regret is doubly painful because of the guilt you feel and the disquieting awareness that you're capable of what you've done. So to avoid the pain, we often neglect confronting it. Maybe we're afraid of what we'll find. Or maybe we're ashamed because we already know.

Yet, as Miami University professor and social psychologist Amy Summerville has argued, even this can be redeemed, especially if cognizance of our failure spurs us on to do better in the future.[3] Regret can also deepen our gratitude and awareness of God's grace. As we were reminded in chapter one, he loved you, chose you, and called you before you were born. He knows your story and the bone-tiring struggles you face. He is mindful of the disgrace you carry, but he still cherishes you, shadow side and all. God empathizes with you as you confront the horror of darkness; his own Son bled and hung on a cross because of it. But as he died, the Lamb slain before the foundation of the world cried out: "Father, forgive them, for they do not know what they are doing" (Luke 23:34).

If you're already forgiven, if the darkest parts of you are already conquered by light, then why not surrender what he's already overcome? Why not renounce your shadows and allow him to bring wholeness to your soul?

If you could get even the tiniest glimpse of the matchless beauty of God's dream for you—of the boundless freedom that's found in the abundant life, of the searing potential you have if only you'd let some things go—if you could just see it, even for a moment, you'd drop everything and never look back.

The heart throbbing behind Peter's words about *self-control* is one of prolific grace and acceptance. God isn't a judgmental, religious killjoy, but a loving Father who only wants your soul to flourish.

REPRESSING YOUR SHADOWS

So how do we experience self-control?

The typical strategy you'll see in religious circles is to emphasize the need to repress whatever sin or struggle you have. Usually this looks like admonitions to throw away, burn, flush, axe, destroy (or whatever synonym best fits) the thing that's causing you to stumble. I've seen sermons where pastors literally smash their computer to illustrate disciplined self-control.

This approach reminds me of Homer's epic poem, the *Odyssey*. When Ulysses tries to resist the bewitching song of the Sirens, he makes his crew tether him to their ship's mast. Technically it works, but as the ship passes by the island and the sound of the alluring melody, he strains so wildly that the bonds cut deep into his flesh. To the other sailors, who had stuffed their ears with beeswax, Ulysses looks insane.

If that sounds fun, you might want to check out the app store on your phone. A few years ago, behavioral economists from the Yale School of Management released an app that virtually binds you to a "Ulysses contract." Here's how it works: You select a goal, such as shedding a few pounds or reading a book, and then you create an incentive to make it happen. It could be a reward, like treating yourself to a night out at an expensive restaurant, or a punishment, like having your credit card pay a hundred dollars to a cause or entity you detest.

And it works!

The app has seen incredible success, with hundreds of thousands of commitments made. In some ways that's not surprising because incentives are often just the push we need to break past unhealthy habits. As Paul said, "The law is made . . . for lawbreakers" (1 Timothy 1:9). He wrote this because rules, contracts, and disciplines are helpful, especially when we're just starting to make worthwhile changes in our lives. As we'll see in chapter 8—disciplines are an invaluable part of shaping character and creating the environment in which our souls can flourish.

Think of a flower bed. You first build the structure to contain the soil, setting up pieces of wood that form boundaries, and then you fill it with the richest soil and fertilizer possible. The work you do ahead of time determines how well the flowers will grow and bloom. So, too, do the disciplines we develop in life, especially early on, determine our soul's health.

> THERE'S A HUGE DIFFERENCE BETWEEN BEHAVIOR MODIFICATION AND DEEP TRANSFORMATION.

But God wants something more than your disciplines: He wants *your heart*. There's a huge difference between behavior modification and deep transformation. While apps, contracts, and smashing computers may be good temporary solutions to generate self-control, there's usually another computer lying around. Or an iPhone. Following Jesus isn't about checking off boxes; it's about growing in love. And when you're in love, you don't have to force it. Love happens.

For example, my wife doesn't threaten me to be with her: "Take me on a date, or else I'll slash your tires." That would be horrible! I *want* to be with her. She doesn't have to persuade me to love her. Besides, after three flat tires, I've learned my lesson.

Your life flows in the direction of your deepest loves. Sociologists tell us that the time when people are most likely to give up habits is when they get engaged, married, or have children. Why? Because their new identity as a husband, wife, father, or mother creates an impulse to rise to that identity. Their love for family trumps everything else.

The secret, then, to self-control isn't simply the "control" part. It's about cultivating a soul that's healthy and rooted in intimacy with God. As you do, watch how you'll begin to thrive and develop the strength and character you'll need to overcome its shadows.

But if your only strategy for self-control is suppression, here's the painful truth: Your life will inevitably broadcast what you're trying to hide. Let's get specific.

RECOGNIZING YOUR SHADOWS

There are different ways your soul will alert you to the fact that something is deeply broken. I call them *shadow symptoms*.

Perhaps the most common shadow symptom is a sense of shame. Shame is the nagging wound of inadequacy and guilt from something left unresolved in your past. But shame is more dangerous than regret. Regret says: "I've done wrong." Shame says: "I *am* wrong." Shame sabotages the hope in your heart that believes you can do better. While regret immediately lets you know when you did wrong, shame comes later. It's the steady accumulation of calcified guilt that can take years to develop but can make itself known at any time. That's why some people will walk into a church and start weeping. It's because—for years—they've been living with a shadow. Like a subterranean spring unable to contain its breadth, something breaks inside, and the need for healing gushes out.

Another shadow symptom can be anxiety. Notice I say *can be*. Many types of anxiety are caused by chemical or neurological imbalances and require medical intervention. I'm not referring to that but to the tension of suppressed shadows—when unconfessed sin, bitterness, trauma, strained relationships, or remorse from a poor decision are unacknowledged or unresolved. You've heard the expression: "A clean conscience makes a soft pillow." But when the dark places go unnamed in our lives, they wedge a gap between who we're projecting ourselves to be and who we know we really are. This can result in things like nervousness, sleep difficulties, inability to concentrate, or overwhelming fears that we'll be found out. We have to work on closing the gap in order to experience inner wholeness, integrity, and the flourishing our souls long for.

A third shadow symptom is anger. Do you ever find yourself easily triggered or overly sensitive? Or do you ever lose it or snap at people in situations, but when you take a step back, you can concede what set you off wasn't a big deal? What is that? Let me introduce you to your shadow. You're projecting your flaws on others because you see them in *yourself.* The Swiss poet Hermann Hesse said the tendency to judge is a form of self-loathing: "When we hate someone, what we hate is something in him, or in our image of him, that is part of ourselves. Nothing that isn't in us ever bothers us."[4]

Again, I think of David after he was confronted by the prophet Nathan for his crimes (2 Samuel 12). Nathan told David about a man who was stealing his neighbor's sheep. Before he even finished, David responded by sentencing the thief to death.

Nathan then replied: "You are the man!" (verse 7).

Don't read it as: *You da man!* This wasn't Nathan giving David a fist bump; he was calling him out. David was ready to execute a guy for stealing a sheep, but he was guilty of something far worse. In life, disparaging others—especially if it's irrational or unwarranted—is probably a shadow revealing a far-reaching problem. Whenever you point a finger, you've got three pointed back at you.

There's also the shadow symptom of self-destructive behavior. This can manifest as promiscuous sexual activity, dangerous risk-taking, self-harm, binge eating, pessimistic self-talk, or compulsive activities like gambling or substance abuse. Not long ago I met with someone who struggled with drug addiction. For years, he had tried various "Ulysses contract" approaches, and they'd all failed. As we spoke, we began to peel back some of the complicated layers of his story, and what we found was heartbreaking. He had been abused as a child, betrayed by a close friend, and experienced a painful breakup. Day after day, he carried with him an overwhelming amount of anguish. The drugs were the symptom, a tactic to cope and numb himself. The real issues were the unacknowledged and unhealed places.

Finally, a symptom many of us struggle with is avoidance. When there are vices we'd rather keep in the dark, or parts of our stories we're ashamed of, we'll instinctively avoid situations that make us feel uncomfortable. We may push people away when they get too close, stay in bed until noon to avoid responsibilities, or resist places like church or communities that will hold us accountable. We don't want to be exposed or judged, so we withdraw.

I recently learned that in the Latin-speaking countries during the Middle Ages, their word for "evil" was *privatio*. We get the idea of privacy from this word. Not that privacy is a bad thing, but the people of the time wisely understood how the more isolated we become, the more vulnerable we are to evil. Sin's greatest asset is secrecy.

Invariably our shadow sides project many more symptoms than these five. But when you look at the symptoms, are any visible in your life? Are there ways in which you're being sabotaged by shame, anxiety, anger, self-destructive behavior, or avoidance? If so, it's a clear sign that something inside you is hurting. There's a shadow lurking nearby, and it's time to drag it into the light.

RENOUNCING YOUR SHADOWS

A good starting place to receive the gift of self-control is repentance. We cannot heal what we refuse to acknowledge. Repentance is not merely saying we're sorry or having moods of remorse; it's verbalizing our urgent need for God, denouncing our shadows by name, and following up those words with action.

TO REPENT IS TO ADMIT YOU'VE LOST YOUR WAY, THEN RETURN TO WHERE YOU LAST EXPERIENCED GOD— WHERE YOUR SOUL WAS ALIVE AND YOU WANTED NOTHING BUT MORE OF HIM—AND BEGIN AGAIN.

Repentance is the voice that calls us back from the dead-end road of self-justification and blame-shifting. That is why, in the Old Testament, the words *return* and *repent* are the same. To repent is to admit you've lost your way, then return to where you last experienced God—where your soul was alive and you wanted nothing but more of him— and begin again.

When David was called out by Nathan, he penned this confession:

Wash me clean from my guilt . . .
For I recognize my rebellion;
it haunts me day and night . . .
Oh, give me back my joy again. (Psalm 51:2–3, 8 NLT)

Can you hear the passion and pain in David's voice? His lack of self-control, and the chaos it caused to himself and others, made him sick. He was desperate to come home.

As many of us have discovered, though, the first step back is usually the toughest. It's been said, "If you board the wrong train, it is no use running along the corridor in the other direction."[5] You need to jump off. Repentance begins with naming where our lies have taken us. And that hurts. A lot. But it hurts a lot more if our lies name us.

I'll never forget a time when I was pastoring on Maui. We lived there for eight years, and I quickly learned that a sizeable part of a pastor's life is to "marry and bury." I just never dreamed that one day I'd do both in the same service.

In Hawaii, the beach is *the* destination to get married—or as the locals joked, *Mauied*. Most weddings were routine and usually very short: *I do. I do. You're done!* But this one was different. The day before, I met with the bride and groom to discuss their vision for the service. We went over the length, location, and order of events, and then they asked if I would be willing to release a live dove as a symbol of their love when they finished their vows. I'd never seen this done at a wedding, but I've learned it's always best to do what the bride wants; and so I agreed. They explained that the dove would be sitting in a picnic basket on the beach. My job was to reach down, take the dove out, say a few words about their vows and "the wings of love," and then dramatically release the bird in front of the guests.

On the afternoon of the wedding, it was sunny, gorgeous, and eighty degrees. A quintessential day in paradise. The little cove where we met was filled with about a hundred guests, and we stood barefoot on the sand looking out over the turquoise water. We began in prayer, I shared some thoughts on marriage, and the bride and groom shared their vows with one another. Then, right on cue, I reached down and gently lifted the dove out of the basket. I talked a bit more about marriage, adding the requested analogy of how they, like the dove, were joined on *the wings of love*. I moved my hands upward to release it.

At first, everything must have looked great. The dove was lifted high into the air. The bride and groom, hand in hand, looked up, beaming with joy. *Oohs* and *aahs* escaped the mouths of friends and relatives. Cameras clicked. But then, in a moment I'll never forget, gravity took hold—and the dove plummeted dramatically back to earth. The crowd watched in disbelief as the bird hit the warm sand with a thud.

The dove was dead. And it had been dead for some time.

Evidently, in transit from the car to the beach, the dove had expired without anyone's notice. I should have suspected something was wrong, but I was too busy speaking to pay any attention.

I've had some awkward moments in my life, but nothing had come close to this. We stood there in a silence that felt like eternity. The crowd was stunned. I literally didn't have a clue what to say. Finally, the bride spoke up. In a very polite, although clearly shaken voice, she asked, "Should we bury it?"

"Of course," I said, relieved to have a plan. I knelt and dug a dove-shaped hole. With everyone looking on, I gingerly placed it inside, covered the dove with the sand, and then stood up.

Thankfully the bride and groom had a great sense of humor, and they broke the ice with a few comments about resurrection. Everyone laughed. I did too.

What started out as a marriage ended in a funeral.

When something is dead inside us, we can try to fake it. At least for a while. Others might think we're soaring and thriving because most of us know how to *act* that way, but we know we're just coasting, living off borrowed momentum and borrowed time. Falling feels a lot like flying but inevitably, *wham!* Gravity wins and then everyone knows we're made of dust.

But the good news is God loves to meet people in the dust. When we name our sin as David did, putting language around our disappointing decisions and cringeworthy secrets, Jesus whispers: *I forgive you.* Not because our sins are irrelevant, but because his grace is infinite.

It's not the absence of failure that makes your soul flourish; it's the overwhelming presence of grace. And you'll know you've encountered it when, like David, you're honest about the lies you hide.

Honesty forces you to grapple with vital questions, motivations, and influences that caused your sin to persist in the first place. Behind every shadow is a substance. Just like when you step outside on a sunny day, the shadow on the pavement projects the contours of you. So, too, your shadows always point to something in your life—an event, a memory, a heartache, a moment of pain or disappointment—that you've been concealing from God, others, and maybe even yourself. True repentance doesn't stop at naming the shadow; it asks the deeper question of how the shadow came to be.

If you go on social media, you'll be inundated with people who, in the name of authenticity, love to talk about their shadows. Influencers and their followers fawn over each other for having the courage to "tell their story." I'm not trying to knock that, but I think there's deeper water to swim in. And here it is: We need to explore what it is about *that* failure that seduces us. Why do we have such a hard time with self-control when it comes to certain issues? What part of

TRUE REPENTANCE DOESN'T STOP AT NAMING THE SHADOW; IT ASKS THE DEEPER QUESTION OF HOW THE SHADOW CAME TO BE.

our story has made us so susceptible to that temptation? Why do we struggle with anger, depression, or self-doubt? Why are so many of our relationships falling apart? Why do we have that compulsion? What in our past causes us to act out in that way?

These are difficult questions, but they're crucial if you want deliverance. Too often, we flatten "confession" to half-heartedly mouthing a list of things we've done wrong. But that's just the beginning. The harder work is asking what the shadows reveal about us. As we begin to honestly engage with those questions, we'll see the true self emerging from under the hardened scales of the false self. Only then will we begin to flourish.

REDEEMING YOUR SHADOWS

Rabbis in the ancient world argued there are two impulses in every human heart. They called them the *yetzer hara* (bad) and the *yetzer hatov* (good). Interestingly, they believed the *yetzer hara* was an energy or force that could actually be redeemed for good in our lives. For example, the impulse toward self-interest, once redeemed, could be used for creative causes, such as building a home or starting a business. The impulse toward greed, once redeemed, could result in wise financial decisions, investments, or saving money. Or the impulse toward passion could lead one to fall in love, selflessly nurture a family, and remain tirelessly committed to one's spouse.

In his enigmatic societal critique *The Marriage of Heaven and Hell*, the English poet William Blake echoed the rabbinic notion that human impulses and energies could be harnessed toward good: "Without contraries is no progression."[6] There's a lot to contemplate there. Now, I don't believe we ought to capitulate to our evil impulses, especially because we're commanded to put them "to death" (Romans 8:13). But I do see in this an invitation to pursue redemptive ways to channel our soul's fire toward holiness, health, and wisdom. Perhaps this clash between our inner heaven and our inner hell represents, in the words of Jungian analyst Robert A. Johnson, "the highest form of creativity" as it galvanizes greater longing for the way of Jesus.[7]

If that's true, maybe it's why God allows certain shadows to haunt us; and why, when we confess sin, the desire for it rarely goes away. We often expect God to thwart us from ever being tempted again. Occasionally that happens. But most of the time, at least for me, I still feel the pull of temptation. Why? One reason is because we still live as flesh and blood. Until heaven, we'll continue to struggle with sin's ugly presence in our lives.

But, secondly, I wonder if God isn't as concerned with repressing our shadows as he is with redeeming them. What if our shadows matter because they bring us to a place of humble dependence? What if he doesn't want to sweep them under the rug but instead expose them for our healing and the healing of others? What if God's intent isn't to airbrush the imperfections in our lives but to beautify them with his forgiveness and grace?

Instead of getting frustrated that God won't take your shadow away, maybe a better question would be: What does a healthy version of my shadow look like? How can I harness *yetzer hara* to bring beauty into the world? How can God use this part of my past to announce resurrection life?

Here's what resurrection means. Every part of your story—the victory and defeat, the laughter and horror, the joys and sorrow—is teeming with possibility. Jesus is redeeming all of it:

Fear redeemed is an opportunity for courage.

Pain redeemed is a catalyst for strength and resilience.

Aggression redeemed is transmuted into Spirit-filled passion.

Addiction redeemed is transformed into disciplined focus.

Regret redeemed is reshaped into compassion and empathy.

And your life redeemed looks like the beauty of Jesus.

Maybe the secret to self-control isn't just about repressing our desires but *redirecting* them to Jesus-centered wholeness. And maybe your soul will flourish, not in spite of your past, but because of it.

Come Alive

To be human is to experience duality. Our deepest selves long for unity with Christ, but as Paul admitted, we still face our shadows: "I see another law at work in me, waging war against the law of my mind and making me a prisoner of the law of sin at work within me" (Romans 7:23). What are some of the shadows in your life? Be specific.

Adding to your faith self-control means getting a grip on the shadows that seek to dominate you. In what ways have you tried to practice self-control? What has worked? What hasn't? Why? How would you distinguish behavior modification and deep transformation?

Your shadows point to and expose dynamics at work in your interior life. As you look at your list of shadows, what do you think they say about you? What are they trying to reveal? In what ways can those shadows be redeemed?

7.

UNSTOPPABLE

And to self-control, perseverance.

—2 PETER 1:6

W hat are you doing tomorrow?"

We had just finished dinner at a friend's house when I noticed a folded newspaper lying next to the sofa. I picked it up and turned to an advertisement that in big letters announced an XTERRA race on the island of Maui. I was pastoring a small church that met on the southern coast at the time. I held the paper up for my friend and then looked closer at the print. The race was the next morning at six a.m.

"So what are you doing tomorrow?" I asked again. He laughed nervously thinking I was surely joking.

"No, seriously," I said. "We should give it a shot! Want to try?"

"Sure, why not?"

Neither one of us knew a thing about XTERRAs; we just assumed it was a breezy jog around a track.

Boy, were we wrong.

The next morning we met at the location given in the newspaper. The place was teeming with athletes stretching, hydrating, and chatting with fellow competitors. Their spandex, toned muscles, neon running gear, and sports watches stood in stark contrast to our dad bods, beach shorts, and cheap tennis shoes. It was obvious they had been preparing for this moment for months, if not years. *What were we doing here?!*

I looked at my friend with unease. We were in way over our heads but still too ignorant to call it off. As we later learned, the XTERRA is "a world-renowned" race, infamous for its difficult terrain, changes in altitude, and grueling trails. Pros fly in from all over the world to participate. Meanwhile, I was just a local pastor who happened to see a newspaper ad after eating pizza.

Someone called out over a loudspeaker that it was time to start. Still not grasping the gravity of what we were about to experience, my friend and I strolled to the starting line. I was struck by how serious everyone suddenly became. They clearly knew what their bodies were about to endure. I rubbed my hands together, took a deep breath, and tried my best to look competitive as we awaited the signal. Moments later the competition began.

The first few minutes were relatively easy as we ran down a paved road parallel to the beach. But then the orange traffic cones that signaled the direction of the race suddenly veered off to the right. Before I knew it, we were on an uneven, rocky dirt path heading straight up Haleakala, the tallest mountain on Maui.

My pace immediately slowed to a pathetic shuffle. Meanwhile, the runners and, most embarrassingly for me, my friend all zipped by me as we ascended higher and higher.

I'm not sure how or why I kept going, but somehow, stumbling and panting, I muddled up the path, then miles later down a lava embankment, across a ravine, and finally back to a two-mile stretch of beach—the final leg of the race. Hours had gone by, and by this point I was exhausted, thirsty, muddy, saturated in sweat, and feeling the weight of how ridiculous it was to show up for an event I'd put zero time into preparing for.

The good news: I "finished" the race.

The bad news: I was dead last in 161st place.

If you've ever done an XTERRA or a marathon, you know what success demands: determination, grit, endurance, tenacity, dedication, and resolve. You also know the demands of preparation—that the key to victory lies not so much in your performance the day of, but in the persistent lifestyle choices you make (and don't make) that bring you to that moment. You can't just win by osmosis; you need to work faithfully to get there.

Peter called this *perseverance*.

Remember, Peter wanted our souls to flourish and our faith to bloom and grow. But he also knew that none of us start our journey fully formed; caring for our souls takes time. Mentorship under Jesus is a lifelong marathon, not an instantaneous, just-show-up-and-expect-to-win sprint. It's for this reason, after introducing the virtues of goodness, knowledge, and self-control, that Peter presented the fourth: perseverance.

THE HOPE OF PERSEVERANCE

Perseverance comes from the Latin word *per*, which means "through," and *severus*, which means "severe." Perseverance is the capacity in your soul to continue even when everything in you wants to stop. Peter

PERSEVERANCE IS THE CAPACITY IN YOUR SOUL TO CONTINUE EVEN WHEN EVERYTHING IN YOU WANTS TO STOP.

mentioned it here because he knew spiritual formation is arduous.

Cultivating your soul takes courage and fortitude. The Bible says it looks a lot like crucifixion: "Whoever wants to be my disciple must deny themselves and take up their cross" (Matthew 16:24). But the Bible also assures us of what awaits when we persevere:

- "Blessed is the one who perseveres under trial because, having stood the test, that person will receive the crown of life that the Lord has promised to those who love him" (James 1:12).
- "Let us not become weary in doing good, for at the proper time we will reap a harvest if we do not give up" (Galatians 6:9).
- "The one who stands firm to the end will be saved" (Matthew 24:13).
- "Let us run with perseverance the race marked out for us, fixing our eyes on Jesus, the pioneer and perfecter of faith. For the joy set before him he endured the cross" (Hebrews 12:1–2).

Let's ponder that last verse for a moment. Jesus endured an unimaginably horrific execution. The best possible man suffered in the worst possible way. But he persevered because he had an unshakable hope: the joy set before him.

This is a valuable insight and one that corresponds with how the ancient world defined perseverance, which they deliberately connected to the word *hope*. In fact, perseverance is literally translated "hopeful endurance." A good example is in 1 Thessalonians 1:3, when Paul wrote the church expressing how thankful he was for them and for their "endurance inspired by hope."

Think back to that doomed XTERRA race I dragged my friend into. Why did I keep going? Honestly, it was because I really didn't have a choice. We were in the middle of nowhere, away from cell service, and I just wanted to get it over with. But there was another motivation too: I knew somewhere out there, past the dirt roads, lava fields, and scorching sun, was a finish line. Water, an air-conditioned house, the sympathy of my wife, and a day recovering on my couch lay gloriously in my future. I had to keep going.

Like Jesus, we, too, live in the hope of heaven. We believe a time is coming when our earthly bodies will be wholly transformed, evil thoroughly vanquished, and God's vision for the renewal of all things perfectly fulfilled. On that day, as the Old Testament prophet Habakkuk attests, God's presence will fill the earth as the waters cover the sea (Habakkuk 2:14).

What an amazing promise! Then, not only will all of creation flourish, so will we.

Occasionally we catch glimpses of what eternity will be like. Think of the things you love about this life: the warmth of the summer sun on your face; laughter with your closest friends; the taste of a hot meal after a long day at work; the thrill of a long-awaited kiss; the feelings of creative flow when you paint, write a poem, or photograph an exquisite landscape; the wonder of holding your child for the first time; or the joy on your relatives' faces when they see your little one taking their first steps on FaceTime. The things you love resonate so much because you're not just bone and blood; you're a living soul. You were made for more. You were made to *be* more. Those things are a tiny foretaste of what awaits in heaven. Those fleeting moments of joy, laughter, beauty, and presence cause the mundane fabric of your existence to be stretched wide. As your faith anticipates the life to come, your soul swells with expectation.

The seven gifts Peter urged us to add to our faith, then, are not just arbitrary suggestions; they're silhouettes of eternity's promise. Heaven looks like goodness, knowledge, self-control, perseverance, godliness, mutual affection, and love. When you choose to receive them, you're furnishing your life with resurrection.

You might think this is an odd place to begin a chapter on perseverance. What does heaven have to do with it? Isn't perseverance just about getting through the struggles of today? I would argue that's more of an outcome. The real power is hope.

The more you envision who God is shaping you to become, the more motivation you'll have to step into the story now.

Hope can also work in reverse. When you consider who you are, or who you've been, you can become profoundly dissatisfied with the landscape of your soul. Have you ever felt like you should be further along in your walk with God? Or frustrated because everything looks hauntingly similar to where you were five or ten years ago? Are you cognizant of an eroding sense of sameness, plagued by the same sins, struggles, perspectives, and habits? I use the word *eroding* carefully because if we're not moving toward new creation every day, we're slowly lapsing into de-creation.

Your truest self is either flourishing or diminishing.

Step back and honestly ask yourself what best describes your soul. Listen to the response it brings. Either way, I know you're thirsty for more of God. He's calling you to higher ground. A. W. Tozer prayed:

> O God, I have tasted Thy goodness, and it has both satisfied me
> and made me thirsty for more. I am painfully conscious of my need

of further grace. I am ashamed of my lack of desire. O God . . . I want to want Thee; I long to be filled with longing; I thirst to be made more thirsty still. Show me Thy glory, I pray Thee, that so I may know Thee indeed. Begin in mercy a new work of love within me. Say to my soul, "Rise up, my love, my fair one, and come away." Then give me grace to rise and follow Thee up from this misty lowland where I have wandered so long.[1]

With this vision in mind, let's zoom in and ask: What does perseverance mean in the trenches of day-to-day life? How is it lived out practically, and how can we "add it to our faith"? Here are three integral ways: discipline, rest, and listening to the right voices.

I. Discipline

The ability to persevere isn't born but made. For some, that's surprising. For example, when we see the stamina and tenacity of XTERRA runners, talented NBA players, Olympic athletes, or gifted musicians, we assume they were "born that way." Even the words I just used to describe them—*talented, gifted*—might lead one to infer these humans have something unusual no one else possesses.

In the book *Grit: The Power of Passion and Perseverance*, Angela Duckworth cited a study by the psychologist Chia-Jung Tsay, who wanted to understand how people perceive musical expertise.[2] Tsay brought in a number of experts and played them two different recordings. They were told the first represented someone who was a "naturally talented" musician, and the other represented someone who had been practicing for years. By an overwhelming majority, the experts said they favored the one who was naturally talented. But here's the catch: The pieces were being played by the exact same person!

Clearly, we're biased to think talent is a matter of innate abilities.

Maybe that accounts for some of it, but recent research has revealed something arguably as important as someone's natural skill set: meticulous commitment to *practice.*

Perseverance, like any other skill, is built up over a lifetime. It's the result of small decisions, steps, and routines. Just as a musician sits down at his piano an hour each day, or a runner gets up at the break of dawn so she can put in a few miles before work, those daily decisions—which may not seem like much in the moment—are building perseverance for when it matters most.

Like a garden, perseverance is the conscientious commitment to plant, water, and cultivate virtue in the soils of your soul. Though the fruit may not come for months or even years, if you're consistent in nurturing your deepest self, you will inevitably flourish.

Thus far we've explored three of the seven gifts: goodness, knowledge, and self-control. How can we persevere in these areas specifically? Let's start with goodness. Since God is the source, then to persevere in it calls for faithfully setting aside time to be with him. So when you wake up in the morning, instead of reaching for your phone to check your Twitter feed, take a few moments to be still before God and invite him into your day. Or, before you go to bed at night, find a quiet place where you can pray and reflect. Thank God for the good things that happened or confess where you failed, and then give him the space to speak truth into your life.

To persevere in knowledge might mean forging a daily rhythm to learn about God and yourself. Angela Duckworth also mentions the Japanese word *kaizen,* which means "continuous improvement."[3] The idea is that each day you're competing with who you were the day before. Time is an opportunity to move yourself forward—making small adjustments, taking incremental steps to perfect your craft, deepening your walk with God, and cultivating your soul through reflection. A good place to begin, as we learned in chapter 4, is to consistently and prayerfully read Scripture and meditate on the ways it intersects with your life. You may also want to set aside time to ask yourself questions about how the day went: *Did I move closer to my goal? What am I grateful for? What did I struggle with? What challenges did I overcome? What improvements can I make tomorrow?* Taking time for *kaizen*, even for a few minutes, will enable you to course-correct toward the version of you that you want to become.

I once heard the story of a rabbi who grasped the importance of this. One night, he stepped outside into the cold and began wandering the empty streets of his town. Several hours later he unknowingly trespassed onto a nearby Russian military compound that was strictly forbidden to civilians.

A soldier called out to him: "Who are you? What are you doing here?"

The rabbi thought for a moment and then asked the soldier, "How much do they pay you?" The soldier told him.

The rabbi responded, "I will pay you twice as much if you ask me those same two questions every day: "Who are you? What are you doing here?"

The reason the questions mattered to the rabbi was because of how they empowered him to identify his calling. So, too, when we daily persevere in knowledge, we're better oriented to understand and establish our life's values.

Intimately related to this is the idea of persevering in *self-control*.

Researchers tell us if we want to break a bad habit, we first need to recognize the steps that led to the habit. For instance, if you struggle with alcohol abuse, be honest about why it's a struggle. What aspects of your past or family of origin have contributed to the desire? What stressors cause you to crave it? What environments does your brain associate with drinking? The weightier issue isn't the addiction but rather what's caused your life to be vulnerable to it. Self-control is learning to identify the problem beneath the problem, and then persevering in making wise, measured choices to break its hold. N. T. Wright has reminded us:

> Virtue . . . is what happens when someone has made a thousand small choices, requiring effort and concentration, to do something which is good and right but which doesn't "come naturally"—and then, on the thousand and first time, when it really matters, they find that they do what's required "automatically."[4]

Perseverance is a "long obedience in the same direction,"[5] and it's forged through our daily, atomic, faithful decisions.

Which brings us back to *The Great Divorce*. In it, C. S. Lewis suggested that heaven and hell exist as by-products of what we do with our choices now. Every decision we make, every act we perform, sets our lives on a trajectory of becoming—either into more warped and twisted versions of ourselves or more whole, radiant versions. At one point on his tour, the narrator observes a ghost of a grumbling old woman and wonders, aloud, why she is there. The tour guide suggests that maybe she is no longer a human grumbler but instead a dehumanized, wraith-like "grumble." It's as if, after years of complaining, the real her gradually diminished, and all that is left is the embodiment of her decisions. Her identity in hell becomes what she did with her freedom on earth.

It's a terrifying thought.

At first, you make your decisions. In the end, your decisions make you.

In this very moment there is something growing inside of you, a seed of potential that, with daily water and cultivation, inevitably becomes *you*. If you choose lust, you're cultivating the soils of a yet-to-be-formed you. If you choose anger, you're plowing furrowed rows into your future. If you choose goodness, knowledge, and self-control, you're sowing seeds of your inevitable flourishing.

Heaven or hell is the realization that every small moment has evolved into the garden you inhabit. According to Lewis, "Everything becomes more and more itself."[6]

> **HEAVEN OR HELL IS THE REALIZATION THAT EVERY SMALL MOMENT HAS EVOLVED INTO THE GARDEN YOU INHABIT.**

2. Rest

A second way to grow in perseverance is through rest. It's ironic, but if perseverance is *the capacity in your soul to continue even when everything in you wants to stop*, then one of the best means of developing it is by learning *when* to stop. In the pre-electronic age, ships periodically needed to recalibrate their compasses by sailing their ships to a still harbor. After a few days the reading on the compass would reset and once again point true north.

In the Old Testament there's a word that reminds me of our soul's need to recalibrate. You'll notice it at the end of certain psalms: *selah*. It can be rendered, "to pause, be silent, or be still."

Selah is the transforming act of withdrawing from the world and allowing God's Spirit to bring into equilibrium all that's been obfuscated in our souls. It permits us to slow down and identify the places he desires to cultivate harmony within. As most of us have learned, it's in the quiet places where God's most enduring work evolves.

Are you pausing long enough to let him shape you for what's next? Do you have rhythms of *selah*? Do you have margins built into your calendar just so your soul can reset? Do you have a Sabbath—a day a week when you step back from your creation to just *be*? As is often said, you're a human *being*, not a human *doing*. Give yourself freedom to allow your mind, body, emotions, and spirit to breathe.

When you allow yourself *selah*—from work, from accomplishing the next pressing task, from the frenetic need to be connected to your smartphone 24/7—your soul has the space it needs to grow fruitful and strong. You'll step out of that time healthier, invigorated, and empowered with a greater ability to endure.

A wide-ranging study done at the Loma Linda University School of Public Health looked at the correlation between having a day of rest, a sabbath, and a person's well-being. According to their research, sabbath "was associated with better mental health and better physical health."[7] Conversely, science reveals failing to rest can have devastating consequences: lowered immunity, headaches, insomnia, muscle aches, and stomach pain. The physical toll of unceasing hurry directly impacts our ability to persevere. In her book *Lean In*, the COO of Facebook, Sheryl Sandberg, recounted the time she interned at a company where a rash of people were quitting. Interestingly they all had one thing in common: unused vacation time.[8]

A painful lesson I've learned about soul-weariness and burnout is that it's usually connected to a nonacceptance of rest. *Selah* has always been hard for me. It's like I have this chronic drive to accomplish—whether that's another talk to prepare, paragraph to write, email to send, person to call back, or project to get ahead of. If I don't have a dozen plates spinning in the air at the same time, I feel guilty. Can you relate? I'm discovering that, at its core, this push to achieve is often pride, an overactive sense of responsibility that manifests in an inability to say no, or an overattachment to perfection and approval—and it's *so* unhealthy. Life inexorably catches up, plates crash to the ground, and if I don't have a deep-seated awareness of who I am apart from what I do, then I'll crash too.

What's scary is that if we don't rest, life will do it for us. And it's way less fun if that happens.

Selah calls out on the other side of our hurry: *Be still*. It's okay to say no, and step away from the pressure to perform. You don't have to run faster and faster just to stay in the same place. You can get off the tread-mill. It's okay to mute all the notifications or put your phone in airplane mode. It's okay to put your feet up with a sci-fi book, take a staycation, go for a long walk, lie on the grass and listen to Hans Zimmer, chillax with some chocolate, soak in a warm bath, or sleep in. Your soul needs a chance to heal. All the other "pressing" things can wait. Mark Buchanan wrote: "Most of the things we need in order to be most fully alive never come from pushing. They grow in rest."[9] If you want to be in it for the long haul; if you want to develop the grit and perseverance to run the race God has given you—embrace the gift of *selah*.

Your future self will thank you.[10]

3. Listening to the right voices

A major factor that determines whether or not we're able to per-severe in life is the voices we choose to listen to. Athletes know this well. When the XTERRA runners took off running up Haleakala, they were buoyed by their families and friends who stood on the side of the road cheering them on and shouting their names. According to science, this affirmation makes a huge difference in athletic potential. Laurie Heller, a professor at Carnegie Mellon University, argues that sound is as requisite as vision, in that it helps players "get completely immersed" in the experience.[11]

Do you remember during the pandemic when NBA players had to compete inside a "bubble"? Without any fans, there was a noticeable impact on their level of play. For example, in a typical season, home teams win about 60 percent of their games. That's largely due to the sheer amount of energy, support, and passion that a crowd brings. The players feed off their spirit, and it inspires them to dig deeper. The NBA knew what a difference it made, so they tried to make up for the absence by piping in the sound of fake cheering. Some arenas even had cardboard or holographic pictures of fans to fill the seats.

But, of course, fabricated applause can't substitute for the real thing. Without any fans present, home teams only won about 52 percent of their games. In the NFL, it was even worse at 49.5 percent. Free-agent defensive end Lawrence Jackson, when asked about the impact of real fans, said: "You attach to that energy, and you want to do something that keeps that energy going. It just takes you to a different level, in the sense that you're not afraid—almost like you're invincible."[12]

The energy you attach yourself to, the people you choose to hear, can either make you invincible or invisible. They have an overwhelming impact on your staying power in your work, school, church, or community. Proverbs 13:20 counsels us: "Walk with the wise and become wise, for a companion of fools suffers harm."

Our life bends to the sound of its loudest voices.

OUR LIFE BENDS TO THE SOUND OF ITS LOUDEST VOICES.

If the loudest voices are encouraging, godly, and life-giving, we'll be more inspired to stay true to God's call for our life. But if we're surrounded by voices that undermine, critique, tear down, or belittle us, it's like death by paper cuts. Over time those wounds cut at your soul until you're ready to quit.

Words create worlds.

You might be thinking, *That's why I feel so discouraged.* Maybe you're in a season right now where the loudest voices in your life are critical: angry emails, bad reviews, bitter parents, jealous coworkers who are positioning for your job. Or maybe it's the noise of secular culture that's working overtime to disciple your soul away from Jesus.

Despite this, it is sometimes possible to lower the volume of toxic voices. Maybe you need to reassess your friendships. Or step away from an unhealthy dating relationship. Perhaps you've been filling your mind with words, podcasts, lyrics, shows, or videos that—if you're honest only make you more discouraged, cynical, or distracted. Can you be more mindful with what you hear?

Sure, I can do better with what I consume; but what about all the negativity, ridicule, gossip, and profanity I hear every day at work, school, or home? They exhaust me. How am I supposed to persevere in my faith when everything around me is screaming that I give up?

We've all had times when we've wanted to give up because of discouraging people and harmful words. I sure have. And to make matters worse, we also face a spiritual enemy, Satan, who shouts in our heads and reminds us of everything we're *not*: not good enough, holy enough, or gifted enough. He's working overtime to fill our minds with lies about God, ourselves, and others.

It's no wonder we're tired.

But I'm learning there's a difference between what you hear and what you choose to *listen* to. Just because something is said *at* you doesn't mean it's *for* you. We don't have to internalize someone else's hate. I know this often feels impossible, but even when every voice in our lives is shouting us down, there's another Voice. A Voice your soul longs to hear. A Voice that first spoke you into existence and whispers your name. A Voice that speaks love, acceptance, compassion, and grace: "He calls his own sheep by name and leads them" (John 10:3).

What does God's voice sound like?

There's a beautiful story in the Gospel of Matthew that gives us a clue. The cousin of Jesus, John the Baptist, was baptizing people in the middle of an arid desert. The Bible says he wore clothing made of camel's hair and a leather belt, and he ate locusts with wild honey. In my mind, he resembles someone from one of the Mad Max movies. Or a thirty-year-old long-haired hipster with a beanie, beard, and skinny camel-hair jeans, washing down a few organic locusts with his kombucha.

People came out to see John by the thousands, including Jesus, who asked John to baptize him. Together they waded into the Jordan River. Matthew 3:16–17 reads:

> When He had been baptized, Jesus came up immediately from the water; and behold, the heavens were opened to Him, and He saw the Spirit of God descending like a dove and alighting upon Him. And suddenly a voice came from heaven, saying, "This is My beloved Son, in whom I am well pleased." (NKJV)

For most of my life, I figured God told him that because, well, he was Jesus. Of course he was "well pleased" with him; he's the second member of the Trinity!

But then, when I encountered the soul-healing prayer of 3 John 2, it completely reframed how I understood Jesus' baptism. The words are worth mulling over again: "Beloved, I pray that you may prosper in all things and be in health, just as your soul prospers" (NKJV).

The same word the Father spoke over Jesus at his baptism, he also utters over you: You are beloved. You are dearly loved. You, the object of his affection, are his delight, his joy.

In you he is well pleased.

Maybe you grew up in a home where you never heard the affirmation of your father or mother. Maybe all you heard was their anger, criticism, or deafening silence. Even now, you're coming to terms with how their words, or lack of words, shaped you. As fantasy writer Patrick Rothfuss wrote: "Everyone tells a story about themselves inside their own head . . . That story makes you what you are. We build ourselves out of that story."[13]

Our lives are built by the voices we hear. It's why they matter.

But God speaks louder. Even if your story has been carved by voices of hate, bitterness, judgment, gossip, or indifference, your heavenly Father thunders: *You belong.*

He speaks identity: *You're my son. My daughter.*

He speaks goodness: *You're forgiven.*

He speaks knowledge: *You're wanted.*

He speaks self-control: *You're free.*

He speaks perseverance: *You're able.*

He speaks love: *You're mine.*

Come Alive

The call to discipleship is a lifelong call to persevere. But Satan, the enemy of your soul, will do everything in his power to tempt you to either abandon your faith or settle for indifferent faith. Are there any areas where you know he is trying to make you give up?

Remember the Japanese word for "continuous improvement" is

kaizen. What steps can you take to continuously improve your soul's flourishing? What steps could you take to help improve the flourishing of others?

Just as a ship recalibrates its compass in still harbors, so, too, do our souls stabilize in times of rest. As you look at your calendar, do you have times set aside to rest? To take a sabbath? If not, how can you reorient your schedule to prioritize it?

As every athlete knows, a key to perseverance is learning to listen to the right voices. Who are the voices in your life that have been most encouraging? Who are the voices in your life that have been most destructive? What steps can you take to tune in the good voices and tune out those that have been harmful?

8.

CASTLES OF THE MIND

And to perseverance, godliness

—2 PETER 1:6

In 2012 news broke about a woman who was reported missing on a tour of Eldgjá in Iceland. A helicopter was dispatched to help find her, along with several vehicles and the Coast Guard. About fifty others scoured the canyon, desperately calling her name and searching for her . . . including the woman herself.

Yes, you read that correctly. She was a devoted member of her *own* search party.

Evidently, she had changed clothes, and when the description of her was read, she didn't recognize who the person was. Hours later, at three a.m., the search was called off "when it became clear the missing woman was, in fact, accounted for and searching for herself."[1]

Someone later quipped how the woman had "potentially done quite well . . . Some people search their whole life and never find themselves."

Someone else tweeted: "Aren't we all, in our own way, this woman?"[2]

That's a little too accurate, more than we'd like to admit.

I could think of several reasons why. Some sarcastic and some philosophical. But the sad truth is that far too many of us move through life without a clear vision of who we really are and who we're becoming.

Take a moment and imagine.

What does the you of tomorrow look like? Ten or twenty years from now, how do you envision yourself? I'm not talking about the job you'll have, how many kids or grandkids you'll have, where you'll live, or whether or not you've paid off your student debt. I'm talking about *you*. I'm talking about the health of your soul.

Every one of us has a self we're forging. What does it look like? Are you more or less anxious than you are now? More or less generous? More or less joyful? Is your relationship with God thriving? How about forgiveness: Are you still fuming about what happened years ago, or have you moved on? Or what about the addictions that you currently battle: Are you free? Are you flourishing?

We may hope for this, but as we all know, hoping and doing what it takes to get somewhere are radically different things. We need to faithfully and intentionally navigate our inner lives into wholeness. The choices we make on this journey may not seem much in the moment, but projected over a life, those small choices become you.

Experts in air navigation know this all too well. They call it the "1 in 60 Rule." It states that for each degree a plane is off target, by the time it has flown sixty miles, it will miss the destination by one mile. A mile may not seem significant, but when you're on a six-thousand-mile flight from San Diego, that one degree will determine whether you're vacationing at an Airbnb in London or adrift on a life raft in the North Atlantic.

Trajectory matters.

What is yours? Do you see where your soul is heading?

Even if you don't, the Bible gives us a practical way to close the gap and get our souls moving in the right direction. It's the word *godliness*—an ancient word we've likely all heard, read, prayed, or sung a thousand times, but maybe never considered the meaning of.

Godliness is also the fifth gift Peter invited us to add to our faith. Let's unpack it together.

THE YOU NO ONE SEES

When you hear *godliness*, what comes to mind? Is it all the sermons you heard in youth group telling you to resist sin and be pure? Is it a character trait in someone you admire? *Wow, look at him; he's so godly.* Maybe it's a way to describe someone you learned about in a book or podcast who sacrificed everything for their faith. Or that friend of yours who faithfully gets up every day at dark-thirty just to pray and read the Bible. She's memorized half the New Testament before you've had your first cup of coffee.

No matter how you define *godliness*, we typically imagine a lofty virtue that's out of reach or someone who looks super religious, devoted, reverent, and righteous. It's like they're on an elite spiritual level, or at least they give off that vibe. They practically live at church, only listen to Christian playlists, and only watch movies that star Kirk Cameron.

It's natural that we think of *godliness* that way, because for thousands of years it was the working definition. In the Greco-Roman world, godliness almost exclusively had to do with someone's *external* religious activity. Godliness comes from two ancient words: *eu*, which means "well," and *sebomai*, which means "to be devout." A godly person was thus someone devoted to the gods; they participated in ceremonies, offered incense at the altar, gave alms, swished bells, and chanted mantras. It was all about appearance—a public religious persona.

The first followers of Jesus, however, had a different vision. They saw godliness not merely as what you do, but who you are. Any hypocrite can act religious, but true godliness flows from the hidden recesses of your inner life: how you concentrate your thoughts, how you reflect on God and the world, how you govern your emotions, and how you cultivate patterns of holiness and integrity. One concordance defines godliness as a "Godward attitude."[3] This mindset endeavors to please him through your every thought.

Let's explore the relationship between godliness and our thought lives.

We can check all the religious boxes—go to church, take in songs and sermons, participate in a small group, tithe, post verses online—but if our thinking is undisciplined, unfocused, or unhealthy, we're no more godly than a Pharisee. In Mark 7:20–23, Jesus warned his disciples:

> "What comes out of a person is what defiles them. For it is from within, out of a person's heart, that evil thoughts come—sexual immorality, theft, murder, adultery, greed, malice, deceit, lewdness, envy, slander, arrogance and folly. All these evils come from inside and defile a person."

In a religious culture that was obsessed with avoiding certain people, foods, or places that could *defile* you, Jesus revealed the source of true sin wasn't external but inside a person's heart and thoughts. To those who had invested their lives in impressing people with external piety, these were difficult words.

Of course, your actions matter, and if done virtuously and consistently, they contribute to the renewing of your mind. (More on that later.) But from God's perspective, godliness is more about the you that no one sees. Like a tree, what's visible to others—the health of the leaves, bark, branches, and fruit—are all a direct result of what's happening at a root level.

GODLINESS IS MORE ABOUT THE YOU THAT NO ONE SEES.

Healthy thoughts are the substrate of a healthy life. Proverbs 23:7 says: "For as he thinks in his heart, so *is* he" (NKJV).

Increasingly, researchers are discovering that your thought life is one of the biggest predictors and influencers of the kind of person you're becoming. Neuroscientists Steven R. Quartz and Terrence J. Sejnowski reveal: "Every nuance of yourself, the very fabric of your experience, ultimately arises from the machinations of your brain. The brain houses your humanity."[4]

This is why the Bible is packed with verses encouraging us to think about what we're thinking about:

- Proverbs 4:26 urges us: "Give careful thought to the paths for your feet."
- First Timothy 4:7 says: "Train yourself to be godly." The word *train* was a military term used by Josephus and other Roman historians to describe soldiers preparing for conflict. Having a healthy thought life isn't something you get by being indifferent; you have to persevere at it. A true woman or man of God is one who has directed their mind in disciplined pursuit of Christlikeness.

- In Philippians 4:7–8, Paul uses another military word when he insists that we "guard [our] hearts and minds in Christ Jesus." How? "Whatever is true, whatever is noble, whatever is right, whatever is pure, whatever is lovely, whatever is admirable—if anything is excellent or praiseworthy—think about such things."
- Romans 12:2 reads: "Let God transform you into a new person by changing the way you think. Then you will learn to know God's will for you" (NLT). Notice how God *desires* to reconstruct the architecture of our imagination. When we allow him to change how we think, *then* we grow in our awareness of his will for our lives.

When our thoughts are healthy, we not only have a capacity to recognize but also to respond to the life God has for us. Your thoughts, like soil, create the environment in which your soul can flourish.

THE YOU YOUR THOUGHTS CREATE

Did you know your thoughts have the power to shape the physical structure of your brain? Every thought you have is an electrochemical event, producing signals that fire information through your nervous system. If certain thoughts occur frequently, connections are formed between neurons that get increasingly sensitive and strong, and eventually they form new receptors and synapses. These neural pathways produce a volume of physiological changes, affecting your emotions, perceptions, energy, sleep, stress levels, and cardiovascular and digestive health. Scientists now believe that thoughts even influence our genetics.[5]

Every moment of every day, your body is responding to the substance of your thoughts. So if you're constantly focused on toxic and negative ideas—how you'll never succeed, how badly you botched a decision, how others gossip about you or dislike you, how underqualified you are, or how you'll never amount to anything—you're carving pathways in your brain that not only make it easier to continue thinking that way but also will influence the kinds of decisions you make in the future. Likewise, if you choose to dwell on the good—the presence of God in your life, his love and acceptance of you, how he has provided for you, protected you, healed you, and called you—those thoughts physically change your neural structure, making you more receptive to identify and experience God's favor.

In my years as a missionary in the South Pacific, I remember discovering a small patch of beach near the school that became my favorite place to read, write, and reflect. Like most of the country even to this day, that part of the island was untouched by twenty-first-century noise. There were no cell phones, busy roads, construction, or clamoring tourists. I remember sitting on the white sands watching the turquoise-colored water as it gently lapped near my feet. Sea urchins filled nearby tide pools, swarms of colorful fish darted in and out of the reef, and occasionally, if I was lucky, I'd spot a manta ray leaping in the distance and then belly flopping in the water with a dramatic splash.

I loved this place. It was my own personal sanctuary.

But when I first moved there, there was no clear-cut path, so I had to forge my own. With a machete, I hacked through the dense bush, prolific vines, and ferns, always on the lookout for poisonous leaves, spiders, or snakes. At first, the path was hard to discern, but in time it became more noticeable. Within a few months, I finally had a little dirt trail that led to my favorite spot on the beach.

Like a path being carved through a jungle, so are your thoughts tirelessly creating new pathways in your brain. Every time you give space and time to a thought, you're conditioning your brain to move in that direction. Soon it becomes second nature. If you focus on anxious, harmful thoughts, you're deepening your neural pathways. Or if you choose to focus on what is uplifting and edifying, you're strengthening those pathways. Just like a river finds the path of least resistance, the flow of your life inevitably rushes toward your most persistent thoughts.

THE FOCUS OF YOUR THOUGHTS DETERMINES THE FRAMEWORK OF YOUR LIFE.

The focus of your thoughts determines the framework of your life.

Repetition becomes reflex.
Reflex becomes routine.
Routine becomes action.
Action becomes identity.

Researchers at Harvard University discovered there's a small but powerful part of the brain called the dorsolateral prefrontal cortex. Think of it as the brain's "pattern seeker." Its primary purpose is to apply guidance regarding the decisions we make in the present while drawing from decisions we've made in the past. In other words, the thoughts we act on, especially those we repeatedly carry out, set a precedent for how we'll act in the future.

If your ritual is to welcome each morning with avocado toast, neural pathways are formed through your brain that establish connections with other parts of your brain, causing you to anticipate said toast the next day. Here's another example. Next time you're waiting to pay for your groceries, look around. Virtually everyone is staring at their smartphones, right? It's because on average, people check their phones within ten seconds of getting in line anywhere. Why is that? It's because we've hardwired our brains to demand digital distraction. That's why we sometimes reach into our pocket thinking our phones are vibrating. Medical professionals call this phenomenon "phantom vibration syndrome." We're so addicted to our screens and the consequent dopamine hits they give us that when we're not staring at them, our brains get annoyed and trick us into picking them up!

Our minds are a jumbled cacophony of well-worn trails. Habits, practices, decisions, impulses, and subconscious reactions crisscross through us—shaping future habits, practices, and decisions. After years and years of reacting to situations in set ways, our responses become pre-programmed, indexing our soul's identities. Thus, when new decisions arise, we simply do what we've always done. Often without knowing it.

You are what you repeatedly think.

I know this can be daunting to come to terms with. It's especially disturbing if you've allowed yourself to acquire deep, unhealthy, negative rhythms of thinking over the years. Sometimes they're so etched into the blueprint of our lives that we don't even realize they're there, or if we do, we feel powerless to change them.

But here's the good news. We *can* change. We *can* evolve. Neurons can rewire. Your brain has a remarkable ability to remap itself. Our mental ruts can get unstuck, and new trails can be forged. Brains are far more pliable than our emotions would have us believe. Elizabeth R. Thornton, a contributor for *Psychology Today*, gives us hope:

> Because of the power of neuroplasticity, you can, in fact, reframe your
> world and rewire your brain so that you are more objective. You have

the power to see things as they are so that you can respond thought-fully, deliberately, and effectively to everything you experience.[6]

You don't have to react slavishly to virulent thoughts. You can revolt. You can rewrite the script, choose more beautiful paths, and create new ways of moving through the world.

How can we begin to do this? How can we apply godliness when it comes to the life of the mind?

Let's consider three practices to live this out: *recognize* unhealthy patterns of thinking, *control* your response, and *replace* unhealthy thoughts with gratitude.

I. Recognize unhealthy patterns of thinking

In 1 Peter 1:13, we read: "Therefore, with minds that are alert and fully sober, set your hope on the grace to be brought to you when Jesus Christ is revealed at his coming." Notice the words *alert* and *sober*. *Alert* was a first-century phrase that meant to "gird up" a toga. Togas were long, flowing robes that—depending on your social class—were sometimes colored with expensive dyes or embroidered with gems and precious stones. They looked striking, but as you can imagine, they weren't practical. If you wanted to go for a hike, play with your kids, or kickbox, a toga seriously got in the way. So in order to free up your legs, you'd *gird up* your toga by pulling the robe to your knees and tucking the excess fabric under your belt.

The word *sober* carries a similar meaning. This isn't just a reference to drinking; it's a call to awareness. *Sober* means to be "awake or alert." Peter was challenging us to be tuned in to the flow of our thoughts, to pay greater attention to the things we allow free rein in our minds, and to liberate ourselves from thoughts that cause us to stumble or be distracted.

In 2 Corinthians 10:4–5, Paul reiterated this concept:

The weapons we fight with are not the weapons of the world. On the contrary, they have divine power to demolish strongholds. We demolish arguments and every pretension that sets itself up against the knowledge of God, and we take captive every thought to make it obedient to Christ.

Because our thought life is a battle, Paul again borrowed a military phrase to depict how to have a godly mind: We "demolish strongholds." A *stronghold* was a fortified defensive or military structure. Picture a medieval castle looming on a hill. Your mind is like that castle. Every thought you choose to dwell on is like a stone in the castle wall. At first, it may seem insignificant—each stone an impulse, passion, or desire—but if you jump ahead years, you've built a castle.

The way to dismantle unhealthy castles in your mind is to "take captive every thought." What does that mean? I remember first reading that verse in high school and musing over how impossible it sounded. *Really? How can I control my thoughts?* On any given day, the average person has sixty thousand of them. Some are wholesome thoughts. Others are harmful or corrosive. How are we expected to *take them captive*?

What it *doesn't* mean is playing mind games, pretending our thoughts aren't there, or forcing ourselves to repress them. That doesn't work. Truth is, it's pretty much impossible. If I asked you not to think of the song "Let It Go" from *Frozen*—well, too late. Now it's stuck in your head, and you probably hate me for it.

2. Control your response

You can't control what thoughts come at you, but here's what you can control: what you do with them when they enter your mind.

Martin Luther is widely attributed to have said, "You cannot keep birds from flying over your head, but you can keep them from building a nest in your hair." It's true that angry, impure, toxic, guilt-ridden, jealous, fearful thoughts will race through your mind on any given day. It's called being human, and you can own that part of your humanity. But you still have the power to determine if you're going to give your mental energy to them.

To illustrate, let's say you walk into the office tomorrow and a coworker gives you a funny look. You immediately feel defensive and wonder: *Why are they mad at me?* At that moment you have a choice: Will you allow that thought to have free rein—inventing all kinds of wild scenarios of why they're mad at you and driving yourself crazy in the process—or will you *take the thought captive* by recognizing that those negative thoughts aren't reality? They might *feel* like reality. But in most cases, it's not the words or actions of people that cause our response; it's our perception and thoughts.[7] Becoming more mindful of your thoughts will free you to respond in a more godly, mature way.

Here's another example. How do you respond when you text someone and they don't text back right away? What goes through your mind? Maybe you don't worry about it: *They must be busy right now. I'm sure they'll get back to me.* Or do you automatically assume the worst? *Why isn't he responding? I can see that it says "read" at the bottom! He told me he was just going to Costco, but it's been over two hours! Did he not know I was waiting for him? Is he meeting someone he doesn't want me to know about?* Five minutes later he walks obliviously through the front door and apologizes that his phone ran out of battery—but for some reason you're still furious with him.

Does any of this sound vaguely familiar?

If you're like me, you know how easy it is for toxic thoughts to take on a life of their own. Fueled by fear, frustration, insecurity, guilt, or resentment, they gaslight your imagination until you affirm their lies. But what is *real* and how you *feel* are two very different things. That's why instead of letting destructive thoughts have unlimited access to our headspace, we ought to step back and discern whether or not the thought has merit.

Ask yourself:

- Why do I feel like this?
- Could I be wrong?
- Could I be misreading, exaggerating, or thinking the worst about this situation?
- What assumptions am I making?
- Is there any evidence that supports these thoughts?
- Are these thoughts true, noble, right, pure, lovely, admirable, excellent, or praiseworthy (Philippians 4:8)?
- Is there a healthier way to interpret what is happening?
- How can I think the best about this person?

We're not always able to take time in the moment to reflect on the nature of our thoughts. That's why we need to prepare our minds for that moment. One strategy is to lay traps for unhealthy thoughts in advance. How? Researchers have discovered that it only takes between five and sixteen minutes a day of calm, meditative thinking to furnish our minds with the capacity to respond to difficult situations.[8] For you, it might mean a time of prayer and self-reflection before you head out the door in the morning. Or sitting in your car and being still in God's presence before you step into the workplace. Or going for a walk in the evening, clearing your mind from the anxiety of the day, breathing out your fears and frustrations, and breathing in God's love and grace.

These simple practices train your mind for godliness. They nurture an environment of inner *shalom* that allows you to respond wisely rather than impulsively and emotionally to the myriad thoughts you have each day. In fact, a study at Oregon State University revealed that those who pray are able to regulate their emotions in a healthier way.[9] When you choose to catch your thoughts, rather than letting them catch and control you, you're not only preventing conflict, destructive spirals, or choices you'd later regret; you're also freeing up mental bandwidth that you can channel toward your flourishing. Caroline Leaf, in her insightful book on the power of our thoughts, wrote:

> In this directed rest state, you focus inward, you introspect, and you appear to slow down; but actually, your mental resources speed up and your thinking moves onto a higher level. When you think in this way . . . you will emerge far ahead of where you would have been if you just operated within the realms of a shifting, shuffling, limited conscious, cognitive mind. This is the state of being still and knowing that he is God.[10]

Stillness tranquilizes the worried, anxious thoughts that ricochet unrelentingly within. It is the sacred hush of the prayerful soul.

3. Replace unhealthy thoughts with gratitude

When you begin to honestly reflect on your thoughts, you may be surprised by how many are disconnected from the *now*. Researchers have found that of the sixty thousand thoughts we have per day, 40 percent are focused on the future, 30 percent are focused on the past, 12 percent are feelings of self-doubt, and 10 percent are worries about our health. That leaves only 8 percent of our thoughts to focus on the present![11]

In my life this is a huge weakness. My wife often tells me I'm like an absentminded professor. I like the professor part; I feel less sure about the absent mind! But she's right. I'm too easily distracted by upcoming events, past events, nonexistent events, things I wish I could do over, conversations I replay in my mind, something I read, a podcast I heard, or a future decision I'm overanalyzing. It terrifies me to think about how much life I've missed out on because of a failure to be *here*.

So, for me, this part I'm about to share comes from a place of vulnerable admission of how far I know I have to go. But, also, it comes from a growing realization of how consequential intentional thinking is. In Colossians 2:6–7, we read: "So then, just as you received Christ Jesus as Lord, continue to live your lives in him, rooted and built up in him, strengthened in the faith as you were taught, and overflowing with thankfulness."

Notice how the words cascade into a vision of flourishing: *live, rooted, built up, strengthened, overflowing.* But it's the last word that really grabs me: *thankfulness.* What I'm learning is that a potent way to have a godly and disciplined mind—one that's less distracted or swayed by worry and more centered and calm—is to practice gratitude.

What is gratitude? It's a posture of the soul, a habit of thinking, that recognizes and honors God as the source of all truth, beauty, and life. Gratitude is the awareness of the miraculous gift of *being.*

When I was a pastor in Hawaii, I'd drive up Haleakala every Monday to write my sermon for the following Sunday. There was a picturesque spot halfway up the mountain where I'd pull over, grab my Bible and notebook, and sketch out the message. Not a bad place to work, and now that we live back on the mainland, I can't believe I took it for granted. One afternoon I could hear some people nearby exclaiming, "Wow! Look at that! Wow!" I jumped up, intrigued to see what they were talking about. Was it a rainbow? Some strange animal? Nope. They were just pointing at the view from the hill. The same view I'd seen every Monday for years.

I realized I had lost my sense of *wow*.

> GRATITUDE IS THE ART OF TAMING YOUR FRENETIC, EDACIOUS MIND TO APPRECIATE THE WONDER OF LIFE AS IT IS RIGHT NOW.

Have you forgotten your *wow*? Are there things, places, opportunities, or people that, in your stress and distraction, you've looked past? Have you failed to see the beauty right in front of you? In the hope of big happiness, are you missing the small joys? God invites you to slow down and fix your thoughts upon him. Gratitude is the art of taming your frenetic, edacious mind to appreciate the wonder of life as it is right now. The fourth-century church leader John Chrysostom astutely discerned, "Happiness can only be achieved by looking inward and learning to enjoy whatever life has and this requires transforming greed into gratitude."[12]

According to the University of Arkansas, thinking grateful thoughts releases the pleasure centers of your brain that make you feel happier. And the best thing? Those feelings of happiness generate a positive feedback loop; you'll be more grateful for them, which only makes you happier![13]

Gratitude also has a direct impact on your physical well-being. Studies have proven that grateful people have fewer medical appointments[14] and stronger relationships.[15] Gratitude bolsters the immune system, decreases blood pressure, heightens energy levels, strengthens the heart, improves emotional intelligence, increases motivation for self-care and physical fitness, and decreases stress, depression, and headaches. Being grateful makes you more hopeful,[16] and it helps you envision a future you that's holistically thriving.

Gratitude is war. Gratitude turns disorder into order and chaos into clarity. It unlocks your perspective and releases you into the fullness of life.

When unhealthy thoughts swarm your mind—envy, anxiety, fear, lust, hopelessness, negativity, comparison, insecurity—choose in that moment to capture those destructive ideas with thanksgiving. You may want to speak gratitude out loud or write it in a journal. What gifts has God given you? How has he provided for you in the past? God is found in rearview mirrors; how has he been faithful in your journey? Then take a deep breath and look around: What is enchanting about this moment? Look closer. You might be surprised. When you're walking with Jesus, a *wow* is never far away.

Gratitude transfigures the world you see.

In the Gospels, just hours before Jesus was tortured and killed, he sat at a table with his disciples. To his left was Judas, who betrayed him for thirty pieces of silver. To his right was Peter, who denied him at a smoldering fire. Jesus took some bread and broke it. He took a goblet of wine and gave thanks. The Greek word for "gave thanks" is *eucharisteo*. For Christians, it's the central symbol of our faith: *eucharist*, or communion. It also contains the word *charis*, which means grace. In an atmosphere tense with the agony of forsaken love, when the disciples' thoughts were manipulated by darkness itself, Jesus literally *gave thanks*; he offered himself.

Gratitude isn't being fake or soppy or pretending everything is okay. It isn't the denial of life's brokenness; it's seeding grace into the brokenness.

In every moment, there is torn bread and poured-out wine. In every dark night, the light of Christ. In every pain, the tender hands of the crucified one. In every anxious thought, an opportunity to whisper our thanks.

Gratitude amplifies the reverence that hums within you. It *adds to your faith* the most beautiful thing of all: awareness of the God who is already here.

THE *YOU* YOU CAN BECOME

Have you ever been curious why, when dogs lie down, they always spin in circles first? My dog, Bella, ceremoniously practices this ancient tradition. I needed to know why, so I looked it up. Turns out it's a vestige of her wolf ancestry. In the wild, wolves would spin before resting to check for predators or to make a bed out of the leaves. So here we are, thousands of years later, and my Goldendoodle, who is about as far from a wolf as instant decaf is from a 100 percent Kona pour-over, spins happily. Not because predators are in our suburban home or she needs to make a bed but because her brain, over years and generations, has been wired to do it.

We're not all that different. Have you ever taken a step back and analyzed why we do the things we do? Why do we lie when the truth is so much more freeing? Why do we stare at our phones before bed even though we know they keep us up? Why do we stress over futile things and miss the beauty of what's right in front of us? Why do we react to the same situations, or the same people, the same way again and again and again?

It's because of how we've coded our brains. The Goldendoodle in us still thinks she's a wolf.

But you can rewrite the script. Starting now.

What we do with our thoughts—how we tend them and channel them—shapes a narrative for our lives. And as we'll see in the following chapter, it can even shape the narrative of our relationships with others.

By recognizing unhealthy patterns of thinking, controlling our responses, and replacing them with gratitude, we craft the story we end up living.

What kind of story is yours?

Come Alive

Let's try this thought experiment again. Imagine your future self ten years from now. What kind of person are you? How are you different from the person you are now? Are you flourishing?

Jesus and the early disciples revealed that godliness is first formed within, beginning with your thought life. Does how you think line up with the person you want to become? Are there patterns of thinking or strongholds you need to dismantle? What are they?

When we choose gratitude, we aren't denying our frustration and pain; we're planting seeds of hope in the midst of those fractured places. Gratitude leverages life's brokenness to allow the light into our minds and thoughts. Take a few minutes and write down some things you're thankful for. A good place to return to is Philippians 4:8. What in your life is true? Noble? Right? Pure? Lovely? Admirable? Excellent or praiseworthy?

9.

CLOSER THAN A BROTHER

And to godliness, mutual affection.

—2 PETER 1:7

It was a warm summer afternoon in Hawaii, and a group of scuba divers and I geared up for a big descent. We were going down 130 feet along a sea cliff near Molokini Island. Most of us were nervous about the sharks—we had heard there were a ton—and it didn't help that our dive instructor called the area "shark condos." I've always hoped that sharks were misunderstood. *Who knows? Maybe they're friendly,* I told myself. And the shark attacks I'd heard about on the news? *Well, who's to blame them? If a guy in a Speedo showed up in your house, you'd probably attack him too!* It's funny how our brains try to rationalize fear.

I slipped on the wetsuit, grabbed my tanks, regulator, and fins, and followed the others as they splashed into the water. A fundamental rule of scuba diving is that you swim with a "dive buddy." It's a way to ensure that if anything goes wrong, you're there for the other person and can watch over their safety. We began our descent, and the surface grew fainter as we plunged farther and farther. Thirty feet. Sixty feet. Ninety feet. Rays of light from the sun penetrated the water and danced around us, then faded into the otherworldly dark blue chasm that yawned ceaselessly below. The beauty was mesmerizing.

Suddenly, at 110 feet, something went wrong. I began to feel a little dizzy and light-headed. Assuming it would pass, I kept descending. Then, without warning, I felt like I was going to pass out. My thoughts were muddled and confused. It was like one of those bad dreams you're trying to escape from. I began sucking oxygen. *Where am I? What am I doing here?* I clenched my teeth as I fought off an irrational urge to pull out my regulator. The last thing I remembered was needing to get my dive buddy. I swam toward him.

And then everything went black.

It turns out I had a bad case of narcosis, a dangerous buildup of nitrogen in the bloodstream. It can cause confusion, anxiety, and hallucinations. My dive buddy, seeing that my eyes were rolled back in my head, grabbed me by the shoulders and ascended to the surface. Next thing I knew I was on my back at the bottom of the boat, squinting my eyes as I tried to adjust to the piercing sunlight. Faces peered down at me, asking if I was okay. My head was reeling as I tried to remember what happened. I wasn't okay, and I probably should have stayed lying there, but I forced myself up and told everyone not to worry.

Half an hour later I wanted to go back down. Everyone thought I was crazy. And, technically, I probably was a little then. But, in my mind, I didn't want to pass up an incredible opportunity to dive. My friend looked at me, puzzled. "Really? Okay, but come straight up if you get dizzy again," he warned. After reassuring him, we got back into the water.

Still feeling the affects from earlier, we decided it was best to stop at seventy-five feet. We began to look around, taking in the dramatic views of the sea cliff, enjoying the serenity that comes from being meters below the world's surface. And then, seemingly out of nowhere, I spotted a massive bull shark about fifteen feet from where we were swimming. He was so close we could see his gleaming white teeth. His black, beady eyes darted back and forth. He clearly knew we were invading his space but didn't seem to mind. And here's the funny thing: I didn't mind either! Normally, I'd be freaked out right about then, but, as luck would have it, a residual symptom of narcosis is euphoria. I felt great! What an opportunity! I got to swim with a shark! Part of me wanted to pet him.

Fortunately, my dive buddy was once again nearby and kept me from doing something dumb—you know, like yanking out an air regulator, snuggling with a shark, or dying.

I'm so thankful he was there, and now I appreciate why people in the scuba world are adamant about having a dive buddy. It can be a matter of life or death.

In the same way, having the right people beside you in life makes *the* difference in whether or not your soul survives or suffocates in hard times. The book of Ecclesiastes reads:

> Two are better than one,
>> because they have a good return for their labor:
> If either of them falls down,
>> one can help the other up . . .
> Also, if two lie down together, they will keep warm.
>> But how can one keep warm alone?
> Though one may be overpowered,
>> two can defend themselves.
> A cord of three strands is not quickly broken. (4:9–12)

Notice how emotionally and unconditionally invested a friend is: If you fall, they don't stand around, pointing out where you fell. They help you back up. If you're cold, they keep you warm. If you're confronted, they're your biggest defender. Friendship is when you have someone in your life who, when you're drowning and gasping for air, is by your side. They don't just throw you a lifeline. *They are your lifeline.*

Little surprise, then, that the next gift Peter said we need to receive for our souls to flourish is *mutual affection.* The word in ancient Greek is *philadelphia.* Yes, it's where we get the "city of brotherly love." It means "friendship, devotion, and tenderness." In Old English the etymology originates from two words: *freo,* which means "free," and *freon,* which means "love." A true friend, then, is one who loves freely.[1] The Celtic tradition devised the term *anam cara,* which means "soul friend."[2] It was how you'd describe someone who gave you affectionate space to honestly confess and uncover the secrets of your heart.

Peter exhorted us to furnish our lives with friends because their affection brings a vulnerability and depth that builds your faith, bolsters your courage, and breaks your fear. Like a mirror, they allow you to see things about yourself you wouldn't ordinarily see on your own.

Friends have the intrinsic agility to draw things out of you that you didn't even know were there. In Old English the word for "friend" is *kith,* which means "knowledge communicated." But it's not merely the knowledge we reveal about ourselves that makes friendship thrive; it's the knowledge friends reveal *to* us. Their zany disposition, biting humor, wit, sarcasm, opinions, and perspectives unmask aspects of your personality that have been there all along but tend to reveal themselves when that person is around. You find yourself laughing more when you're with them. Or dancing more. Or thinking more. Or maybe angry more, in which case you may want a different friend!

Friendship brings an inner wholeness that nothing else can (which explains why, when you lose a friend, you also lose a part of yourself). When you're loved in such a way you can authentically be you—heart open, words transparent, with no secrets, agendas, or ego—your soul feels safe. No, more than safe; you're *accepted*. In a world where it's increasingly hard to trust, where competing voices clamor to sell you their product, engage with their profile, further their ambition, and promote their narrative, a friendship unconditionally whispers: *You belong*.

It's that sense of belonging, I imagine, that will make heaven dazzling. When you belong, you can breathe. You can rest. In the presence of God, every soul will be open, clear, and loved. Those around you will draw out more of your soul's beauty. Can you imagine how rich this eternal perspective will be? Each person will radiate something we could never see on our own, of ourselves, others, and God. Like going from 2D to 3D, heaven will magnify the truth we always suspected: "Christ in you, the hope of glory" (Colossians 1:27).

Maybe that's why genuine friendships can feel so much like heaven now.

THE GIFT OF FRIENDSHIP

What makes friendship so unique is that it's voluntary. You're not forced or obligated to keep your friends. Friendship isn't a contract; it's a commitment. It's a relationship where the only strings attached are the ones you *choose* to tie. In that way, it's unlike any other relationship, like the ones you have with coworkers, acquaintances, people you follow online, or even relatives. As Proverbs 18:24 says, "There is a friend who sticks closer than a brother."

Wait a minute. How could a friend stick closer than a brother? At the

end of the day, isn't it your flesh-and-blood family, your relatives, those
who share the same last name, who will be most loyal and fight for you?

That may or may not be true. And even if they "love" you, they
may not *like* you. Just because you have the same blood in your veins
doesn't mean they automatically have your back.[3] As the comedian
George Burns once said: "Happiness is having a large, loving, caring,
close-knit family . . . in another city."[4]

If you laughed at that quote, you probably know what it feels
like to be a stranger in your own home. Someone I know once joked
that God gave him friends as a way of apologizing for his family!
That may ring true for you. But even Jesus felt alienated from his
family at times; they even denounced him for being "out of his mind"
(Mark 3:21). Later, when they were outside demanding to speak, Jesus
pointed to his disciples and said, "Here are my mother and my brothers" (Matthew 12:49).

Friendship is a commitment fueled by determined love. And that's
what Jesus' friends were to him. Although the large crowds dwindled,
and his own relatives deserted him, his true friends followed him to the
end—as he wept in the garden, was whipped
by a Roman flagellum, and then was finally
crucified between two thieves. Some stood at
a distance. Others, like John, lingered at the
foot of the cross while he breathed his last.
They weren't perfect friends, and far too often
their faith wavered, but they loved him. And
Jesus loved them too: "I no longer call you
servants . . . I have called you friends" (John
15:15).

**FRIENDSHIP
IS A
COMMITMENT
FUELED BY
DETERMINED
LOVE.**

If anyone could have lived without friends,
it would have been Jesus. He was God, after

all. He was in fellowship with the Father and the Spirit. He also knew the deficiency of human love and how susceptible we are to betrayal, gossip, and leaving when times get hard. But still, modeling for us a healthy way to be human, Jesus chose to live his life in community.

We cannot flourish without others. Our soul needs friends like our body needs air.

In a culture that idolizes sexual relationships, this message of friendship is often lost. If you go online and read the latest celebrity gossip, what do the headlines say? Look, These Two Just Became Best Friends! Nope. It's always: Here's Who's Sleeping with So-and-So! Or, to catch your eye, they may say they're sleeping with someone *else's* best friend. But even then, the part that jumps out to us is the sex part.

In a hypersensual, individualistic, insanely busy culture, we've ignored—or at best, redefined—what friendship is. We tend to view friends as an option if we have time for them, or something brought into existence when we press the Follow button. Friends take a backseat to our careers, romantic interests, hobbies, or sports. Not that those things don't matter, but sadly, many of us have friendship so low on our list of priorities that we can go years without having any. We might have acquaintances, people we know at work, or interact with online, but we live with impoverished souls because we fail to recognize the unique and beautiful gifts God has given us in one another.

In the end, you may regret how you loved your hobbies, toys, pursuits, and jobs, but you'll never regret how you loved your friends.

> **WE CANNOT FLOURISH WITHOUT OTHERS. OUR SOUL NEEDS FRIENDS LIKE OUR BODY NEEDS AIR.**

As professor and priest Henri Nouwen recognized, you'll also never forget how they loved you:

> When we honestly ask ourselves which persons in our lives mean the most to us, we often find that it is those who, instead of giving advice, solutions, or cures, have chosen rather to share our pain and touch our wounds with a warm and tender hand. The friend who can be silent with us in a moment of despair or confusion, who can stay with us in an hour of grief and bereavement, who can tolerate not knowing, not curing, not healing and face with us the reality of our powerlessness, that is a friend who cares.[5]

The beauty of their love, as it flows through them and toward you, is how it heals both you and them. Friendship is love made visible.

THE NEED FOR FRIENDSHIP

Did you know the Bible begins by uncovering our aching need for friendship? Personally, I've always found it humorous, and a little disconcerting, that when God made the world, he shouted over all creation: "It is good!" But when he created the first man, he said: "It is *not* good!"

But that's only the first part of the verse. Here's what God said: "It is not good for the man to be alone. I will make a helper suitable for him" (Genesis 2:18).

Did you see that? God created the first human, placed him in a garden, but immediately identified something was deeply wrong. He was lonely and needed a helper. The word *helper* has all kinds of negative connotations today. We envision someone subservient, like an apprentice who hands an electrician a wire cutter or an assistant *to* the regional manager. But the word (*ezer* in Hebrew) literally means "life-saver" or "rescuer." It's used in other places in the Bible, such as when Israel was being besieged by enemies and they put out a desperate call for help. We also see it in other verses to describe God, who comes alongside us when life is falling apart. Husbands, there's a reason we say she's our better half. She literally is.

Adam had it all. An eye-popping garden. A world free from the ugliness of sin. A vibrant relationship with God as he walked with him in the cool of the day. But still, there was something missing. In spite of everything Eden had to offer, his heart yearned for more: friendship with another human.

Sometimes we overspiritualize the idea of friendship. We read about the friend that sticks closer than a brother and say, "Jesus is that friend!" Or we repeat worship songs about how we don't need anyone else but God. Or we turn the Bible's description of friendships like Ruth and Naomi, David and Jonathan, or Paul and Timothy into mere analogies. Baked into our Christian sub-culture is this false idea that the only relationship that matters is our relationship with God. But the verses about Adam needing Eve or Proverbs' description of close-knit friends or the myriad other passages about companionship aren't metaphors. They're describing what it means to flourish as a human. We need the tangible, physical, *with-us* proximity of others to be most fully alive. It is not good for us to be alone.

As so often happens, science is beginning to catch up with the Bible's ancient truth. In recent years, hundreds of studies by scholars and researchers have confirmed the importance of friendship. What they've discovered is fascinating:

- **FRIENDSHIP MAKES YOU HEALTHIER.** When you examine biomarkers such as blood pressure, BMI, and inflammation, they found that those who have reliable friendships were much healthier than those who didn't. A 2012 study from the Netherlands found that a key risk for dementia and other cognitive disorders is loneliness, but those who had thick social bonds were at a much lower risk.
- **FRIENDSHIP EXTENDS YOUR LIFE.** On average, those who foster strong social relationships are less likely to die prematurely than those who live isolated lives. In fact, one study revealed that the effect of friendship on your life span is double that of exercising!
- **FRIENDSHIP HELPS KEEP YOU MOTIVATED.** We've all experienced this: If your friend starts a diet or spiritual practice, reads a compelling book, or suddenly gets into CrossFit, it's only a matter of time before you lose weight, pray, read, and find yourself sweating in the same gym. Study after study has shown that what motivates your friends inevitably motivates you. The opposite is also true. If your friend is cultivating destructive habits, you are 57 percent more likely to go down the same path: "Bad company corrupts good character" (1 Corinthians 15:33).
- **FRIENDSHIP HELPS YOU NAVIGATE GRIEF.** When you go through things like unemployment, foreclosure, divorce, disease, death, or a pandemic, a key factor in your soul remaining healthy is the depth and quality of your friendships.[6] A true friend doesn't just wipe your tears, they help you cry. The way they love "at all times" anchors you in every season (Proverbs 17:17).

The more we learn about the psychological, emotional, and physical benefits of friendship, the more we discover that friends aren't just nice to have around. They're a soul-necessity.

CULTIVATING FRIENDSHIPS

There are two kinds of people reading this. For some, when you hear about the power of friendship, a smile fills your face and your heart beats with joy. You have friends like this, and they've made all the difference in the world. You're even tempted to text them right now: "This chapter is all about you!"

For others, however, this chapter leaves you with a dull ache. You long for authentic friendship. Even now, you're longing for someone who truly knows you, cares for you, and can fan your heart into a flame again.

A TRUE FRIEND DOESN'T JUST WIPE YOUR TEARS, THEY HELP YOU CRY.

Many of us, particularly after the turmoil of the last few years, feel this way. As I shared earlier, a record 67 percent of Americans are lonelier than ever. Perhaps you just moved, started attending a new church, began your first year in college, or have a new job. In seasons like that, it's not uncommon to feel out of place or alone. So here's the question: How do we cultivate friendships? How do we find and foster relationships that are genuine, deep, lasting, and life-giving? Let me offer a few thoughts.

Be Open

This point is a lot harder than it sounds, especially if your attempts at making friends in the past have been rejected or met with blank stares. Anger or tension you can handle; but indifference is the coldest enemy of all. When we're rejected, our natural response is to withdraw behind walls to shield our true self.

While this may seem the best way to insulate your soul from pain, it's also how it dies.

To love is to trust. To trust is to risk. To risk is to live.

Sometimes, in order to come alive to the story we were made for, we need to open our hearts to the question: What if God wants to forge new friendships in our lives? Maybe there's someone you recently met at the gym or church, but because of past experiences, you're not really open to moving past "I'm fine, how are you?" Or maybe someone at school came up to you after class to start a conversation, but you brushed them off because it just seemed like too much work to try. Maybe you struggle with feeling cynical and sarcastic toward others. You know the agony of betrayal, and you're not willing to give them your time.

But what if true friendship awaits beyond your fear? What if God wants to bring you genuine community, intimacy, laughter, connection, solidarity, and affection? It may look different than you thought. When Mary came to the tomb Easter morning, she thought Jesus was the gardener. She could scarcely see him through her tears. But then he spoke her name: "Mary" (John 20:16).

What if God is whispering your name through unexpected people? The guy at the desk you scurry past every morning at work? The woman at Starbucks who makes your latte? The neighbor you've only just waved at for fourteen years? You think they're just the gardener, but maybe they are Jesus in disguise.

Let down your walls. Be open to the possibility of loving again.

Pursue

Proverbs 27:9 teaches us that true friendship "is as sweet as perfume and incense" (NLT). Thousands of years later, we can drive to Macy's if we want cologne, but when this was written, these things were the rarest of treasures. Perfume was the wealth of queens. God is reminding us that friendship is a treasure to be valued and cherished. And like any treasure, if you want it, you have to dig deep to find it.

Too often we want to outsource friendship to luck and chance, or we put unrealistic expectations and pressure on others to make it happen. (*If they want to be my friend, they need to prove it.*) But true friendships are a by-product of intention. As Proverbs 18:24 challenges us, a person who has friends "must himself be friendly" (NKJV).

Friendships are forged on two-way streets of mutual giving—sharing memories, moments, and unstilted words. All the while, pausing to listen—not simply to respond but to comprehend. Friendships are never hurried. They flourish in the empathetic space of nurturing the needs, hopes, and anguish of the other.

The architecture of friendship is time. Year by year, as you invest into their life, you'll build a holistic framework and awareness of who they are. You'll understand: How are they wired? What brings them delight? What burns their heart with sorrow? Are they thriving emotionally, mentally, and physically? Are they flourishing in their walk with God? Are they making wise choices? If not, you'll be willing to call out the ways they're making a wreck of their life. "Faithful are the wounds of a friend" (Proverbs 27:6 NKJV). The most loving friends are those who care enough to confront; they don't just say what the other person *wants* to hear, but what they *need* to hear.

By the way, that's how you'll know who your real friends are. Anyone can be there for you in your success, but a true friend steps up in your ruin. Look around the next time you stumble. Who is there for you? Whose hand is reaching out to raise you to your feet? Real friends don't just point out your failure. They stoop down to redeem it.

Friendship is relentless pursuit of one another's flourishing. As the Norwegian writer Arne Garborg is credited to have penned: "To love a person is to learn the song that is in their heart and to sing it to them when they have forgotten."[7]

Is there anyone in your life who may have forgotten they are loved? A mother, father, son, or daughter? A roommate or someone at work? Chances are someone you know is struggling with their identity. What would it look like for you to remind them of who they are: cherished, treasured, valued, loved?

The song you sing to others—through words, deeds, prayers, and time—lavishes more hope than you could ever know.

Forgive

If you're looking for a friend who never shows up late, forgets, spreads rumors, or lets you down, you're probably looking on the wrong planet. Because we're all flawed people, sooner or later everyone disappoints. The question isn't *when* will our friends hurt us, but how will we react when they do? Cicero once said that friendship "is a kaleidoscopic and complicated thing."[8] Indeed it is. Because friendship is "knowledge communicated," your heart is susceptible to what your friends do with that knowledge. If they turn it against you, gossip, or stab you in the back, our ecosystem of trust collapses and our hearts reel from the pain.

The simplest option is to cut them off. Over lunch, someone once told me how he dealt with a strained relationship. "Two words," he said. "Unfriend, block." The problem is, true friendships aren't digital avatars; they're gardens. The roots are expansive, roping and intertwining around and within the soil of your life. You can try to rip them out, but their presence tarries. Your thoughts return to them. Things remind you of them. Hurt turns to anger, which turns to bitterness, and bitterness is the poison that contaminates your soul.

Hebrews 12:15 warns: "See to it . . . that no bitter root grows up."

Doesn't it seem like *everyone* is bitter right now? Bitter about politics, economics, the pandemic, the climate, social issues, you name it. I've witnessed relationships devolve into name-calling over masks. I've seen churches become increasingly tribalistic, using the pulpit to denounce groups of people instead of sharing the hope of the gospel. I've seen online mobs gang up to shame and *cancel* people.

In our cultural quest for justice, we've forgotten grace. We've forgotten how to love, listen, learn, empathize, and forgive. And when someone does or says something we disagree with, we excise them from our lives.

This scorched-earth approach to relationships only isolates us more and undoubtedly has fomented our nation's current epidemic of loneliness. If you're just looking for someone who thinks, acts, looks, speaks, and votes like you, it's not another person you're describing, it's *yourself.* But friendship isn't found in mirrors; it's found in the celebration of difference.

I'm more convinced than ever that if we want our land to heal, we need a revolution of grace. And that starts with us and how we engage with the people in our lives. Before cutting someone off, take a deep breath and ask: Am I holding on to something I don't have to? Is this disagreement worth breaking a friendship over? Is it worth burning that bridge?

In some cases it is. Perhaps they're lethal to your soul's health. Maybe their words or actions have irrevocably destroyed your capacity to trust. The best thing for you might be to move on.

But you can still forgive.

Forgiveness doesn't mean the instant restoration of trust, that you approve of their actions, or that you sugarcoat what they did; it means intentionally releasing bitterness. It's a way of saying *What happened no longer controls or dominates me. I'm liberating my soul so it can flourish.* Corrie ten Boom, who survived the Holocaust while seeing those closest to her brutally murdered, wrote: "Forgiveness is the key that unlocks the door of resentment and the handcuffs of hatred. It is a power that breaks the chains of bitterness and the shackles of selfishness."[9]

Forgiveness is a choice that eventually becomes a feeling. At first the key is hard to turn and easily gets jammed in its rusty lock. But as you *will* your heart to forgive, moment by moment, day by day, the chains gradually give way to the freedom of grace. In time, the friendship may even resurrect into something more beautiful than you can imagine.

Or maybe it won't.

But can you still appreciate the role that person played in your life? Some friends are lifelong; you met them when you were in second grade, they were in your wedding, and you'll probably be with them someday playing bingo in a retirement home. But other friends are for a season. They were around for a period of time, but now they've drifted to the margins.

But can you still cherish the time that you had?

As you look out on the garden of your life—and although those people aren't as prominent now but are somewhere among the lush and distant memories—can you appreciate how they once touched your heart?

Things are different now. You've changed. They have too. But that's okay.

You're just glad they were there.

And for those who've been with you through thick and thin yet still love you and stand with your soul—who hear you without saying a word, who accept you with all your quirks and oddities, who share your joy and grief—treasure them well. They are heaven's grace. They are God's gift, and the most meaningful gift you could give yourself. A true friend is God's way of sewing up your wounds and reminding you: "You are not alone."

So when life tries to break you, open your heart to receive their compassion.

And should they stumble or stray, pursue them with indomitable grace.

And when necessary, forgive. And don't stop forgiving.

Because any who walk with you on the unpredictable, grueling road of life, who obstinately stand with you through all of its chaos and pain, they are a true *anam cara*: a friend for your soul.

Come Alive

Who are your closest friends? Make a list of those who have been "lifelong" friends, then others you've had for shorter seasons. Sometimes it's painful when friends drift in and out of our lives, but we can still appreciate how they impacted us. Take a moment and thank God for each of these friends by name. As you pray, share specific ways they helped your soul flourish.

Friendship isn't accidental; it's intentional. Are you open to new friends in this season of life? What are some practical steps you can take to cultivate new friendships? Inviting them over for a night of food and games? Meeting up this week over a cup of coffee? Asking them to share their story with you?

Is there anyone in your life you feel angry or bitter toward? Ask God to help you forgive. Romans 12:18 says, "If it is possible, as far as it depends on you, live at peace with everyone." Notice the phrase "if it is possible." Some relationships cannot heal. Nor, especially if they've been dysfunctional or abusive, should they. However, in those relationships God is calling you to reconcile, what part do you have to play? Maybe it's as simple as a thoughtful text letting them know you're thinking about them, that you're sorry about how things turned out, or that you're still there for them. Go ahead. Do it now.

10.

BETWEEN TWO FACES

And to mutual affection, love.

—2 PETER 1:7

Will Norman, a cancer survivor in Texas, had just endured the most difficult year of his life and was struggling to find someone to talk to about it. Rather than focusing on his own pain, he decided to do something quite unusual—help others through theirs. Will set up a "listening tent" in the parking lot of a liquor store with a banner that read "Need to talk? I'll listen." Sitting in one of two chairs under the tent, Will invited anyone to talk confidentially and without judgment about whatever they wanted to discuss.

The response was overwhelming. Even today, strangers sit there with Will sharing their struggles, grief, and hope. One man told Will he was on his way to kill himself. Will urged the man to seek help and he did. A week later, when he was released from the hospital, he stopped by the tent again—this time to express his gratitude. As he was leaving, he suddenly turned and said, "I love you."

"I love you too," Will replied.[1]

Why does Will sit in that tent day after day? What motivates him? In his own words, "No one can help everyone, but everyone can help someone."[2]

Love looks like a lot of things.

Sometimes it's creativity: witnessing the joy that comes through unexpected surprise. Sometimes it's lament: giving meaning to others' pain through your tears. Sometimes it's laughter: because their happiness is indispensable to your own. Sometimes love looks like compassion. Or vulnerability. Or mercy . . .

Or sometimes it's just listening.

Presence, I think, is the apotheosis of love: lingering just a little longer because someone's hurting or alone.

THE WAY OF LOVE

Jesus was once asked a question that he answered with a single word: *love*. The story is found in Matthew 22, when the Pharisees confronted him: "Teacher, which is the greatest commandment in the Law?" (v. 36). They wanted to test Jesus' theology with the intent of wielding it against him. Also, asking a rabbi back then to condense commandments into an elevator pitch of a sentence or two was fairly common.

For example, Rabbi Hillel, who lived a century before Jesus, was once approached by a man who stated he would convert to Judaism if Hillel could summarize the entire Torah while he stood on one foot. Hillel replied: "What is hateful to you, do not do to your neighbor."[3]

When Jesus was asked, however, he took it a step further. Instead of focusing on hate, he shifted the emphasis to love:

> "'Love the Lord your God with all your heart and with all your soul and with all your mind.' This is the first and greatest commandment. And the second is like it: 'Love your neighbor as yourself.'" (Matthew 22:37–39)

Jesus made it staggeringly simple. The way to become a flourishing, whole, beautiful human is through receiving and practicing the gift of love. As the Russian novelist Leo Tolstoy wrote in *War and Peace*: "Love is life. All, everything that I understand, I understand only because I love. Everything is, everything exists, only because I love."[4]

Look around. See how the earth announces the love of God. Look past your iPhone screen with its cluttered apps; past your office space and its incandescent bulbs; past the subways, frenzied roads, and neon signs; and notice *creation*. Look at the trees, the hills, the lakes. Do you see the dazzling array of color, the craftsmanship and detail, how the land blossoms in beauty? Notice the stars, how they're at once sublime and understated, yet also dauntlessly shouting *purpose*. Observe the people around you; see their dignity, their uniqueness, their *otherness*. Despite insecurities and eccentricities, they all, in some mysterious way, reflect the image of God.

Every gift in your life exists because God, who is love (1 John 4:8), eternally and generously pours himself into the world.

In Genesis, love became a word—*Let there be*—and creation was born. When Jesus appeared, the word became flesh, and creation was reborn. And now this God of endless giving invites your soul to flourish by adding to your faith the greatest virtue of all: love.

You've likely heard that the ancient Greeks had four words for love, but the truth is that when you study the writings of the Greeks, especially Plato and Aristotle, you'll discover there were actually seven:[5]

- *Storge*, meaning "affection," describes your love for a family member—or if you're a parent, how you feel about your kids.
- *Philia* is the love you have for a casual friend or someone you admire.
- *Eros* was used for erotic, sensual love. In Greek mythology, *eros* was like an arrow unleashed from Cupid's bow that caused people to fall feverishly and irrationally in love.
- *Ludus* is similar to our words *tease* or *flirt*. Like swipe-right apps, it focuses on seductive conquest rather than commitment.
- *Pragma*, where we get our word *pragmatic*, is all about mutual goals rather than romantic interests. It often emerges in struggling and passionless couples who only stay together for the sake of appearance or financial stability.
- *Philautia* is self-love. It can manifest in healthy ways such as confidence and self-esteem, or it can devolve into egotism and hubris.
- *Agape* is the seventh and purest form of love. Agape is different from the other loves in that it's unconditional. It doesn't depend on emotions, how it's reciprocated, or whether or not it makes practical or financial sense; it just freely gives. Agape is resolute love without manipulation, creatively breaking your life and heart open for the sake of others.

Agape is how God loves you. And it's the word Peter used when he invited us into a flourishing life: *add to your faith agape*.

GENEROUS LOVE

Practicing agape is complex, especially in a culture like ours where we don't even have a clear understanding, or agreement, of what love is. Over the last five years, "What is love?" has been a trending search on Google. Some see love as a feeling—a sensation fueled by desire, chemistry, or how attractive the person is. But if love is just feelings, then what about the morning you wake up and don't have any? That sounds more like infatuation—thinking you've found someone flawless. But real love is when you realize they aren't, yet you're there for them anyway.

Others define love as tolerance. One of the most pernicious lies of mainstream culture is that if you love someone you must blindly acquiesce to every choice they make, or if you disagree with their lifestyle, you must hate them. But that's a false choice. You don't have to compromise your beliefs to be loving. Love doesn't merely tolerate people; it fights for people. It speaks up when people go down destructive paths, then walks patiently with them in pursuit of healing. Love isn't blind, it sees imperfections, weakness, and flaws . . . but then intentionally shells out grace.

Secularism and naturalism reduce love to a chemical chain of events. It's purely biological—the collision of neurons and hormones in your body that creates the illusion of "loving" another person. Some scientists even suggest that love can be physically controlled, much like we use antidepressants to control mood. I even heard that some are exploring the development of medicine that could affect how we feel and experience love.[6] Can you imagine? You're in an argument with your husband. You can either sulk all day or drop a pill in his coffee. After a couple sips: "Wow, honey, I love you. You're amazing.

You're gorgeous. I'm wrong, and you're always right." Some of you are searching online right now for this pill!

In addition to our culture being deeply confused about the nature of love, we also face another hurdle: narcissism. The word *narcissism* first emerged from the Greek myth of a handsome hunter named Narcissus. Renowned for his physical beauty, he drew the attention of countless female admirers but spurned them all. One day, he discovered a clear pool of water, and for the first time saw a reflection of himself. He was so captivated by his appearance that he immediately fell in love. For the rest of his life, he hovered at the edge of the pool, mesmerized by his own reflection until he eventually died. After his death, a flower bearing his name sprouted through the ground.

Have we become a culture of narcissists? Some social scientists believe we have and point to narcissistic personality traits that have skyrocketed since the 1980s.[7] In one study first developed in the 1960s, people were asked if they considered themselves to be "important." At that time, only 12 percent said yes. Thirty years later, the same study was conducted, and that number had risen to 80 percent!

This may be partially due to economic factors and the postindustrial shift toward individualism. Or technology that has made it possible to work with less interaction or dependence on others. Or social media, with its attention-seeking selfies, hyperemphasis on follows and likes, and algorithms that study and parrot your opinions. Our digital echo chambers often deafen us to the needs, struggles, and perspectives of others. While these platforms claim to connect us, they may be eroding our capacity for empathetic, give-and-take interactions.[8] Like the guy who was talking nonstop to someone he knew: "Okay, enough talking about me. Let's talk about you. What do *you* think about me?"

What's tragic is that our obsession with self is only making us more miserable, anxious, and depressed.[9] The more inward and self-focused we are, the more our souls collapse from the weight of ungiven love. To love is to give. To flourish is to grow *outward*. The bigger we are in our minds, the smaller we actually become.

That's why Scripture repeatedly urges us to shift our focus away from self to others:

- "Strive to do what is good for each other and for everyone else" (1 Thessalonians 5:15).
- "Be kindly affectionate to one another with brotherly love, in honor giving preference to one another" (Romans 12:10 NKJV).
- "Make my joy complete by being like-minded, having the same love, being one in spirit and of one mind. Do nothing out of selfish ambition or vain conceit. Rather, in humility value others above yourselves, not looking to your own interests but each of you to the interests of the others" (Philippians 2:2–4).

Notice how Paul connects joy with generous, selfless living. I once heard someone say that *joy* is an acronym: *Jesus. Others. You.* In that order. That doesn't mean we ought to neglect our needs or desires; in truth, Jesus told us to love our neighbors *as ourselves.* He probably said this because self-love comes naturally to most of us, and we therefore have a frame of reference for what he's talking about. The challenge is the *neighbor* part.

Selfishness and pride detest living outward: serving, sacrificing, putting the needs of others ahead of ourselves. But because we were created in the image of a generous God, we know there is no more satisfying way to live. Did you know that the word *generosity* comes from a Latin word meaning "noble birth"? If you were the son or daughter of a generous king, it was expected that you would be generous too. Not simply because of who you knew, but who you were.

That is why the most generous people you meet aren't necessarily those who give the most; it's those who give of *themselves*. It's the single mom who works two jobs just to provide for her kids. The barista who chooses to stay late so an exhausted coworker can go home. The waitress who goes out of her way to make a family's meal unforgettable.

Through quiet, thoughtful, creative acts such as these, you inevitably discover that what you gain far outweighs any amount of cost.

In the words of Jesus, "It is more blessed to give than to receive" (Acts 20:35). If you remember from chapter 2, the word *blessed* means to flourish. And Jesus isn't just talking about the happy feelings you get after leaving a large tip. He's talking about a *lifestyle* of generosity that produces flourishing at every level: emotionally, spiritually, mentally, and even physically. Researchers at the University of Zurich concluded that generous people have better health, lower blood pressure, lower stress, and higher life expectancy.[10] Other studies reveal that helping others releases happiness chemicals in the brain, feeds optimism and satisfaction, reduces feelings of loneliness, and inspires others to help people too.[11]

Psychologists use the word *elevation* for the warmth people experience when they witness someone else's kindness. In fact, just *hearing* about a loving act is often enough to motivate a person to do the same.[12] Agape is contagious. "Pay it forward" is more than a cliché; it's deeply efficacious. Every time you help someone in need—showing compassion, giving your money, sharing your resources or time—you are literally making your life, and the lives of those around you, look more like Jesus.

When you think about the people you know who have the most radiant souls—those who are the most hopeful, gracious, benevolent, and kind—what do they have in common? I promise one characteristic they don't share: *selfishness*. The most beautiful people are those who choose to make their lives beautiful for others. As Thomas à Kempis wrote in his classic, *Of the Imitation of Christ*, their whole being broadcasts sacrificial love:

> Love is a great thing, yea, a great and thorough good; by itself it makes every thing that is heavy, light; and it bears evenly all that is uneven.
>
> For it carries a burden which is no burden, and makes every thing that is better, sweet and tasteful.[13]

PRACTICING LOVE

Agape love is a choice that expresses itself in generous action. In the Old Testament, there is a wonderful word that weaves these ideas together: *tzedakah*. It's a combination of "love" and "justice."[14] In English, there isn't an equivalent for *tzedakah*. Maybe it's because we view love and justice as competing values. But in ancient Israel, to love *was* to practice justice. That's why you'll find so many verses about donating to the poor, allocating wealth such as crops and fruits, showing hospitality to immigrants and refugees, or pooling resources to share with others. They believed they were closest to the heart of God when their lives emanated his love.

It's even possible Israel built their place of worship with this truth in mind. Their most sacred piece of furniture in the sanctuary was called the ark of the covenant. On top of the ark was the *kaporet*, or mercy seat. It was the place where the high priest offered sacrifices and met with God. According to Exodus 25:20, on either side of the mercy seat were two cherubim: carved angelic creatures whose faces were turned to one another. The late Rabbi Jonathan Sacks suggested this little detail is rich with meaning: *"God speaks where two persons turn their face to one another* in love, embrace, generosity and care . . . We discover God's image in ourself by discerning it in another."[15]

I hear echoes of this insight in Paul's promise that someday we will see God "face to face" (1 Corinthians 13:12). But in a very real way, we can also see him now, in the face of one another. Every time you selflessly serve, charitably give, patiently wait, silently listen, graciously invite, and passionately intercede—you'll know that God is near: "Whatever you did for one of the least of these brothers and sisters of mine, you did for me" (Matthew 25:40).

Like Israel's sacred ark, God dwells between two faces.

I think that's why, when Jesus walked our earth, people were so instinctively magnetized to him. He personified *tzedakah*. As they drew near, they encountered a generous king.

Jesus didn't go about life aloof and untouchable. He was physically invested in the flourishing of others. His heart led him to the lost, lonely, and marginalized. He made their grief his grief, their pain his pain, their wounds his wounds. Although large crowds pushed and clamored around him, Jesus was never too busy to notice one weary traveler who needed rescue. He never looked past people; he looked *at* people. Fully present, fully engaged, his only focus was whoever was standing right in front of him: The paralyzed man at the pool of Bethesda. The sightless man in Jericho. The guilty woman caught in the act of adultery. The exhausted lepers on the road to Jerusalem. The bleeding woman who desperately clung to the edge of his clothes.

The very people the Pharisees and self-righteous did their best to avoid, Jesus went after. He ran to those the religious ran from. He broke bread with the sinner, spent time with the forgotten, loved the outcast, carried the weary to rest. As they drew close to him, their souls came alive. Because, as we unearthed in chapter two, flourishing is *participation in the life of God*.

In him, every longing of the heart found its home.

Do you remember Jesus' words when he stood on the mountain? *Blessed are the poor. Blessed are those who mourn. Blessed are the persecuted. Blessed are the hungry and thirsty* (Matthew 5:3–12).

If Jesus were to give that sermon today, it would probably sound something like this:

> Blessed are the single moms, the orphans, and widows, for you are the future of God's new creation. Blessed are those who have made a train wreck of their lives, and those burdened by the weight of shame, guilt, and regret, for God is on your side. Blessed are the dropouts, addicts, unemployed, indebted, anxious, and depressed, for you are the object of God's affection. Blessed are those who don't have it all together, those who have run out of strength, ideas, and will-power—because yours is the kingdom of heaven.

To all who felt unwanted, burned by religion, or abused by systems of power— Jesus gave them a place to belong. And throughout the world, he's doing the same today.

Religion condemns the broken. Jesus makes the broken his mission.

Religion excludes the sinner. Jesus invites them to his table.

Religion shames people for having dirty feet. Jesus kneels down to wash them.

How does he do this?

RELIGION SHAMES PEOPLE FOR HAVING DIRTY FEET. JESUS KNEELS DOWN TO WASH THEM.

Through you. Through me.

I was once introduced to a couple from our church who found a beautiful way to love others. She was originally from Iran but was forced to flee the country because of intense persecution against her and her family. Following Jesus came with a great cost, but rather than diminishing her love for him, she was brimming with ideas to convey his love to others. She and her husband started a community garden in their backyard and opened it up to people living nearby. She reached out to refugees who were struggling to adapt to their new life in the United States, and they began to work the soil with her. Friendships were formed. She shared her story and how God's love had transformed her life, and their lives were transformed too. Through the simple act of gardening, the refugees found acceptance—the kind that Saint Francis of Assisi described by saying: "We have been called to heal wounds, to unite what has fallen apart, and to bring home those who have lost their way."

How about you? Who are the people God is calling you to love?

VISIBLE LOVE

When Jesus condensed all the commandments to loving God and loving our neighbor, a religious leader asked a follow up question: "Who is my neighbor?" (Luke 10:29). To the ultra-pious in that culture, a neighbor was typically defined as someone who was on the same team—politically, ethically, and socially. It's easy to love people like that, isn't it? But what made Jesus so revolutionary, and what got him into all kinds of trouble, was how he radically redefined *neighbor*. A neighbor, according to Jesus, wasn't just an insider, political ally, or someone with a worldview you deemed acceptable; it was the outsider.

It was the people you had a hard time getting along with, disagreed with, or despised.

Who is my neighbor? Jesus proceeded to answer the man's question by telling him the parable of the Good Samaritan.

Wait a minute. *Good* Samaritan? Right off the bat, Jesus was offending social mores. Because of some serious bad blood that went back hundreds of years, Jews and Samaritans in the first century *hated* each other. As far as the religious leader was concerned, there was no such thing as a good Samaritan. The term was an oxymoron. It would be like someone saying, "There was once a good terrorist who walked down the street kicking puppies."

But it gets worse.

The way Jesus told the story, the Samaritan was the hero. He said there was a man beaten up and left for dead on the edge of a road. Several people noticed him lying there, but the priests and religious leaders, too busy to notice or care, drifted to the opposite side and kept walking. Only the Samaritan stopped to help the dying man. He bandaged his wounds, put him on a donkey, and transported him to an inn where he was fed and cared for. The Samaritan covered all the expenses and more.

When Jesus finished, he asked who the neighbor was to the dying man. You can hear the reluctance in the religious leader's voice: "The one who had mercy on him." Jesus said, "Go and do likewise" (Luke 10:25–37).

"Go." Agape love is never stagnant. It does things. It goes places. It seeks out the desperate without relenting. It draws near to the sinner without condemning. It sits in the darkness without despairing.

Love agonizes in prayer where the world is in pain.

When Peter said *add to your faith agape*, he wasn't just saying love the lovely or love the people you agree with. Or even love the people in your life who are easy to love. That's more like *philia* or *storge*. But agape intentionally pursues those you would label a Samaritan—those who aren't a part of your politics, network, or tribe. It's the people who grate against your nerves and irritate you, who you'd rather avoid at the office or leave ghosted online. You know, the person who, when you hear *they'll* be at the party, gives you plenty of reason not to go.

Those are the people God has called you to love. Jesus said:

> "If you love those who love you, what credit is that to you? Even sinners love those who love them. And if you do good to those who are good to you, what credit is that to you? Even sinners do that. And if you lend to those from whom you expect repayment, what credit is that to you? Even sinners lend to sinners, expecting to be repaid in full. But love your enemies, do good to them, and lend to them without expecting to get anything back. Then your reward will be great, and you will be children of the Most High." (Luke 6:32–35)

These are some of the toughest words ever spoken. But they're also some of the most hope-filled and redemptive. Choosing to generously love someone you'd rather hate, or at best ignore, can be excruciating. And, literally, it is. The word *excruciating* comes from the Latin *crux*, from which we derive *cross*. Agape looks like Calvary—wooden beams, jeering crowds, stretched-out hands, unfeigned forgiveness. When you choose agape, it can feel a lot like death. But the cross always leads to resurrection and an empty tomb.

Relationships can heal. Enemies become neighbors. Samaritans become friends.

And even if your love is rejected, it's okay. Love is its own reward. Agape isn't determined by the one receiving, but by the one who chooses to give.

THE GOD OF LOVE

On my office wall at work is a replica of one of my favorite paintings, *Girl with Balloon* by the street artist Banksy. On the left, it depicts the tragedy of love and loss, but on the right are scrawled the words: "There is always hope." Banksy, who keeps his identity secret, is famously idiosyncratic. The *Telegraph* calls him "mad and creative."[16] His paintings are often provocative, subversive, and politically charged. They've appeared on bridges, walls, and streets all around the world. When I say "appeared," they really do. He will show up in a city, and at some point in the night, covertly go to work on a building he chose to make a canvas. In 2020, just in time for Valentine's Day, the city of Bristol awoke to a mural of a young girl firing a slingshot of flowers at a wall.[17] Another night that year, he tagged the inside of a train on a London subway.

In 2018, the original *Girl with Balloon* was put on auction. It sold for 1.4 million dollars. But the moment the gavel hit the podium, the painting suddenly began to drop into a shredder Banksy had built into the bottom of the frame. Art connoisseurs watched in horror. People have speculated whether Banksy was making a dramatic statement about consumerism or how money is the death of art. But what's striking about the story is how the person who bought the work reacted. They asked her if she still wanted it. I think most of us would decline. But, surprisingly, she said yes.

Guess how much the painting is worth now? Almost twenty-five million dollars. Its value has soared. Currently, the pieces are on display at a popular museum in Germany. The auction house that originally sold *Girl with Balloon* put out a statement: "In the process of destroying the artwork, a new one was created."

Sometimes the most breathtaking art emerges from what life has shredded to bits. God knows this, and maybe that's why he never gives up on creation. It's certainly why he never gave up on us. Although we've marred and fractured his image, violated our integrity, abandoned our promises, betrayed our values, and misplaced our hope, he still accepts us, gathers up the broken pieces of our lives, and calls us beautiful.

The gospel is about a God who abandons everything, rushes to the other side of the road, pulls us into his arms, clothes us with grace, and welcomes us home. As Frederick Buechner exclaimed in one of his sermons, "Turn around and believe that the good news that we are loved is better than we ever dared hope, and that to believe in that good news, to live out of it and toward it, to be in love with that good news, is of all glad things in this world—the gladdest thing of all."[18]

YOUR LIFE IS THE STORY GOD IS WRITING FOR A LOVELESS WORLD.

When you encounter God's agape love, when his grace crashes through the built-up layers of your heart—shattering your coldness and fear, dissolving your shame, and flooding you with hope—you can't help but share its redeeming power with others. Agape is impossible to contain.

Love is a story in search of expression. And your life is the story God is writing for a loveless world. John 15:12 says, "Love each other as I have loved you." He created you, gifted you, empowered you, and called you—not just for your own flourishing but for the flourishing of others.

THE RISK OF LOVE

When you begin to see life through the prism of outward-directed love, your capacity for wonder multiplies. It's a wonder to celebrate

God's beauty in others. It's a wonder to see redemption at work in them: how his Spirit renews, how his grace restores, how his mercy heals. It's a wonder to witness new creation bursting amidst the ruins of the old. Paul called it a fathomless mystery: "For God, who said, 'Let light shine out of darkness' made his light shine in our hearts" (2 Corinthians 4:6).

And the greatest wonder of all is that God invites *us* to be a part of this process.

When my family and I moved to Portland, Oregon, I remember stepping into an empty townhouse with sparse-looking walls and an even sparser budget to furnish it with. So, naturally, we brought the few dollars we had to a yellow-and-blue Swedish temple: IKEA. A couple hours later, we were back home with some boxes of plywood, I mean furniture, that I spent the afternoon putting together. At that time, my daughter was seven, and wanted to help. Of course, I knew if she got involved, the building process would go a lot slower.

And it did.

But as she fumbled around with the screwdriver, and I with the nuts and bolts, we eventually finished the task. Perfectly? Not even close. But we had fun. We laughed. We jumped on Styrofoam. We made airplanes out of the instruction manual. The room was a mess, and I loved it. Building memories trumps building bookcases every single time.

I can't help but wonder if God feels the same about us. He's creating something in this world, that when you see it, you'll want to join in. Ask him. He wants nothing more than to say *yes*. For sure, you'll mess up on the way, forget the instructions, and lose a bolt or two, but that's what grace is for. Besides, God has way bigger aspirations than how well you perform; he's healing this world through love. And love is never about efficiency, rules, or obligations. It's about relationship.

Intimacy. Compassion. Time. It's about slowly cultivating the flourishing of those you're with.

Michelangelo, perhaps history's greatest sculptor, once remarked how he was able to design such exquisite works of art: "In every block of marble I see a statue as plain as though it stood before me, shaped and perfect . . . I have only to hew away the rough walls that imprison the lovely apparition to reveal it."[19] Michelangelo saw something inside stones that no one else could see—a masterpiece—and through careful, patient taps of his chisel, he revealed what he knew was there all along.

For reasons only fully explained by love, God sees something in you that emulates him. He sees goodness in you, knowledge, self-control, perseverance, godliness, mutual affection, and love. He sees possibility. He knows how you languish for the flourishing life. At times, you may look at your life and only see a shadow of your former self. God looks at you and sees a shadow of your future self.[20]

Even now, in subtle and often not-so-subtle ways, the divine Sculptor is at work in you, refining you, smoothing off the rough edges. He sees a masterpiece in you and is going to set it free. As James K. A. Smith wrote:

> Jesus is a teacher who doesn't just inform our intellect but forms our very loves. He isn't content to simply deposit new ideas into your mind; he is after nothing less than your wants, your loves, your longings . . . To follow Jesus is to become a student of the Rabbi who teaches us how to love.[21]

Here then is our calling and the secret to a flourishing soul: Live in love. Pursue the wanderer. Embrace the fearful. Rescue the orphan. Bind up the wounds of the fallen. Call the outsider your neighbor.

Show mercy to the doubter. Welcome the homeless home. Lavish grace on the sinner. Live so your love makes nonbelievers question their disbelief in God.

Every act of love unveils the nearness of God.

Every step of love brings close the presence of God.

Every choice of love whispers: *He is here.*

Love answers the world's longing with unremitting hope: *Your longing has a name. It's Jesus.*

LIVE SO YOUR LOVE MAKES NONBELIEVERS QUESTION THEIR DISBELIEF IN GOD.

Come Alive

To love is to invest in another person's flourishing. When we choose to love, which requires getting our eyes off ourselves and dying to selfishness, our souls come alive too. Why do you think that is? Why do we flourish when we focus on others?

In your opinion, what is the difference between love and tolerance? Why does our culture confuse the two?

One of Jesus' practical metrics for love is how we love our neighbor. How about you? Do you know your neighbors? What are their names? What are their needs or struggles? How have you shown love to them? If you haven't, think of a creative way you can love them this week.

THE STORY YOU
WERE MADE FOR

*What you are is God's gift to you, what
you become is your gift to God.*

—UNKNOWN[1]

A number of years ago I read a surprising yet true story about a police officer in Lindale, Texas, who received a call from a real estate company reporting a stolen house. *What?!* He assumed, as I first did when I read it, that it was a trailer. But it turns out that it was actually a house made of brick. The officer jumped in his car and drove down to the neighborhood. He couldn't believe what he saw: a nearly vacant lot with a pile of rubble littered on what used to be someone's unused home. He began to investigate and later discovered that a couple of guys, over the course of three months, slowly dismantled the house, selling the parts for drugs. Plumbing, kitchen fixtures, doors, and windows were all loaded into trucks and sold. The neighbors, meanwhile, figured it was a construction project. "It's the strangest case I've ever worked in my life," the police officer said. "Everybody drove by and waved at them."[2] And why did they do that? Because the job was done so slowly and methodically, onlookers thought everything was legit and hardly noticed when a wall or two went missing.

Like that Texas house, we are all in the process of becoming.

Through our actions, words, disciplines, and habits, we are either creating a greater wholeness or a greater disintegration in our thoughts, our words, our relationships—our *souls.*

What we repeatedly do, we become.

We see this with athletes whose ethos of disciplined excellence empowers them to perform at otherworldly levels. Or surgeons who operate on the wounded with elegant, healing precision. Or communicators who transform labyrinthian ideas into a simple rush of words that mobilize a crowd. Or skydivers, like Luke Aikins, who leap twenty-five thousand feet without a parachute onto a suspended net.

We all appreciate excellence when we witness it in others. And it's not merely what they bring to their craft that we find so compelling; it's the brick-by-brick commitment it took to get them there to begin with.

In 2 Peter 1:5, we're urged to "make every effort" to build our faith. Why? First, because Peter was mindful of the impulses and powers that seek to dismantle us. Second, he knew from experience that when we commit to cultivating life's greatest and most incalculable resource—our souls—the outcome is flourishing.

Not just in this life. But in the life to come. In that sense the passage we studied isn't simply a liturgy of the soul; it's an eschatology for the soul. Peter was furnishing us with the building blocks for the kind of future God wants us to inhabit.

Day by day, however you choose to develop or diminish yourself will influence what you'll carry with you into eternity. Maybe this is why Jesus spoke so often of "talents," "rewards," and investing our treasure in eternal things. This very moment, and for as many moments as you have remaining on this earth, you're constructing your soul's identity.

What shape is it taking now?

As we've explored the seven gifts God offers, we've seen their beauty, their possibility, how they each build on the other, and how they each build within us the framework and promise of a deeply flourishing life. I should also mention that they're profoundly synergistic: The more you receive and practice them, the more natural and enlivening they become. This is a characteristic and consequence of any virtue or vice. The more you do a good act, the easier it gets to repeat. The more you do a bad one, the easier it gets to repeat. It's how habits are formed. It's how people are formed. And it's how eternity is experienced.

Your soul is a gift from God.

Tend it well.

And may you, brothers and sisters:

Make every effort to add to your faith goodness; and to goodness, knowledge; and to knowledge, self-control; and to self-control, perseverance; and to perseverance, godliness; and to godliness, mutual affection; and to mutual affection, love. (2 Peter 1:5–7)

Through the power of the Holy Spirit, let's go, live it out, and come alive to the story you were made for.

ACKNOWLEDGMENTS

I am so grateful for those who helped breathe this book into life.

For my wife, Elyssa; you are the most beautiful soul I know. Even through your season of grief and loss, you've fearlessly embodied faith, hope, and love. For my daughter, Amelia; you never cease to make me smile, laugh, and be astonished at the wonderful woman you're becoming. For my parents, for teaching me how vital the life of the soul is. For my father-in-law, Mike; you're an incredible man of God. I'm grateful for our long hikes, theological conversations, and games of chess.

Thank you to Gerry Breshears for your wise mentorship and Phil and Diane Comer for the way you've faithfully encouraged me. Louis Neely, you have been unceasingly kind and generous; thank you for being such a wonderful friend and pastor.

There are seasons in every life when one's soul becomes heavy from weariness. But true friends are faithfully present to help carry that burden and fan your soul back into flame. I am beyond grateful for those who have reignited my soul in difficult seasons. You are my *anam cara*—and I thank God for your presence in my life:

Christopher Kenney, Zach Vestnys, Bryan Fowler, Matt Heverly, Jim Wright, Glyn Brown, Daniel Fusco, Jan and Jim Bisenius, and Edward and Roman Ozeruga.

Finally, I want to thank the insanely gifted team at W Publishing: Debbie Wickwire, Kyle Olund, and Paula Major. Thank you for believing in this project, encouraging me, and inspiring me in countless ways. And my agent, Bill Jensen—it's been an honor working with you. I've learned so much from you, not only about the complicated and evolving world of book publishing but also about operas and symphonies. (I think we're due for another show, by the way.)

NOTES

Leave the Parachute

1. Maquita Peters, "Skydiver Luke Aikins Sets Record for Highest Jump Without Parachute," National Public Radio, July 30, 2016, https://www .npr.org/sections/thetwo-way/2016/07/30/488083554/luke-aikins -becomes-first-person-to-jump-from-a-plane-without-a-parachute.

2. Maggie Astor, "Skydiver Survives Jump From 25,000 Feet, and Without a Parachute," *New York Times*, July 30, 2016, https://www.nytimes.com /2016/07/31/us/skydiver-luke-aikins-without-parachute.html.

3. Daniel Defoe, *Religious and Didactic Writings of Daniel Defoe: The Compleat English Gentleman; And, of Royal Education*, eds. W.R. Owens and Philip Nicholas Furbank (United Kingdom: Pickering & Chatto, 2006), 205.

Chapter 1: Step Into the Story

1. Lisa Colón DeLay, *The Wild Land Within: Cultivating Wholeness Through Spiritual Practice* (Minneapolis, MN: Broadleaf Books, 2021), 16–17.

2. David Hajdu, "Wynton's Blues," *Atlantic*, March 2003, https://www .theatlantic.com/magazine/archive/2003/03/wyntons-blues/302684/. I would like to credit Matt Heard for first introducing me to this story

in a sermon and later in his book, *Life with a Capital L: Embracing Your God-Given Humanity* (Colorado Springs: Multnomah, 2014), 197.

3. SingleCare Team, "Stress Statistics 2021: How Common Is Stress and Who's Most Affected?" SingleCare, January 27, 2021, https://www .singlecare.com/blog/news/stress-statistics/.

4. Michael J. Breus, "Why Are Americans Always Sleepy?" *Psychology Today*, March 26, 2020, https://www.psychologytoday.com/us/blog /sleep-newzzz/202003/why-are-americans-always-sleepy.

5. Chris Melore, "America's Toughest Year? 3 in 4 Say 2020 Pushed the Country into an 'Existential Crisis,'" StudyFinds, December 17, 2020, https://www.studyfinds.org/americas-toughest-year-2020-left-people -feeling-defeated/.

6. Chris Melore, "Lonely nation: 2 in 3 Americans feel more alone than ever before, many admit to crying for first time in years," StudyFinds, April 29, 2021, https://www.studyfinds.org/lonely-nation-two-thirds -feel-more-alone-than-ever-many-cry-first-time/.

7. "48% of Americans are feeling down, depressed, or hopeless during the COVID-19 pandemic," USA Facts, September 22, 2020, https:// usafacts.org/articles/45-americans-are-feeling-down-depressed-or -hopeless-during-covid-19-pandemic/.

8. Dan Witters and Jim Harter, "In U.S., Life Ratings Plummet to 12-Year Low," Gallup, April 14, 2020, https://news.gallup.com/poll /308276/life-ratings-plummet-year-low.aspx.

9. "Harvard Youth Poll—41st Edition: Spring 2021," Harvard Kennedy School, Institute of Politics, April 23, 2021, https://iop.harvard.edu /youth-poll/spring-2021-harvard-youth-poll.

10. Thomas Moore, *Care of the Soul: A Guide for Cultivating Depth and Sacredness in Everyday Life* (New York: HarperCollins, 1992), xi.

11. Adam Grant, "There's a Name for the Blah You're Feeling: It's Called Languishing," *New York Times*, April 19, 2021, https://www.nytimes .com/2021/04/19/well/mind/covid-mental-health-languishing.html.

12. Martin Heidegger, *Being and Time*, trans. John Macquarrie and Edward Robinson (Albany, NY: State University New York Press, 1996), 189.

13. Alec Tyson, Cary Funk, Brian Kennedy, and Courtney Johnson, "Majority in U.S. Says Public Health Benefits of COVID-19 Restrictions Worth the Costs, Even as Large Shares Also See Downsides," Pew Research Center, September 15, 2021, https://www.pewresearch.org /science/2021/09/15/majority-in-u-s-says-public-health-benefits-of-covid -19-restrictions-worth-the-costs-even-as-large-shares-also-see-downsides /?utm_content=buffer94e7b&utm_medium=social&utm_source =twitter.com&utm_campaign=buffer.

14. Marlando D. Jordan, "Spiritual Life: Choose to Have a Healthy Soul and Prosper," *Tri-City Herald*, March 18, 2017, https://www.tri-cityherald .com/living/religion/spiritual-life/article139572563.html.

15. Online Etymology Dictionary, s.v. "languish," accessed September 21, 2021, https://www.etymonline.com/word/languish.

16. William Shakespeare, "Those lips that Love's own hand did make (Sonnet 145)," Academy of American Poets, https://poets.org/poem /those-lips-loves-own-hand-did-make-sonnet-145.

17. Saint Augustine, *Confessions*, trans. Henry Chadwick (New York: Oxford, 2008), 278.

18. Brennan Manning, *The Ragamuffin Gospel* (Colorado Springs: Multnomah, 2005), 90.

19. John Newton, "Amazing Grace! (How Sweet the Sound)," https:// hymnary.org/text/amazing_grace_how_sweet_the_sound.

20. Eric Betz, "Is the Multiverse Theory Science Fiction or Science Fact?" Astronomy.com, December 14, 2020, https://astronomy.com/news /2020/12/is-the-multiverse-theory-science-fiction-or-science-fact.

21. Robert Farrar Capon, *Between Noon and Three: A Parable of Romance, Law, and the Outrage of Grace* (Grand Rapids: Wm. B. Eerdmans, 1997), 72.

Chapter 2: To Be Fully Alive

1. Naomi Levy, *Einstein and the Rabbi: Searching for the Soul* (New York: Flatiron, 2017), 11.

2. Fyodor Dostoevsky, *The Brothers Karamazov*, trans. Constance Garnett (New York: Modern Library, 1995), 282.

3. Ruth Haley Barton, *Strengthening the Soul of Your Leadership: Seeking God in the Crucible of Ministry* (Downers Grove, IL: InterVarsity Press Books, 2018), 24.
4. John Ortberg's book *Soul Keeping* was extremely helpful in researching this chapter—particularly "Part I: What the Soul Is." John Ortberg, *Soul Keeping: Caring for the Most Important Part of You* (Grand Rapids: Zondervan, 2014).
5. Dallas Willard, *Renovation of the Heart: Putting on the Character of Christ* (Colorado Springs: NavPress, 2002), 199.
6. Todd Wilson, "The Integrated Pastor: Toward an Embodied and Embedded Spiritual Formation," in *Tending Soul, Mind, and Body: The Art and Science of Spiritual Formation*, eds. Gerald Hiestand and Todd Wilson (Downers Grove, IL: InterVarsity Press Books, 2019), 111.
7. Jamie Laughlin, "Satellite of Love: Dario Robleto's Art Sounds Like Humanity at Its Best," *Dallas Observer*, July 13, 2016, https://www.dallasobserver.com/arts/satellite-of-love-dario-robleto-s-art-sounds-like-humanity-at-its-best-8481258.
8. Eva M. Krockow, "How Many Decisions Do We Make Each Day?" *Psychology Today*, September 27, 2018, https://www.psychologytoday.com/us/blog/stretching-theory/201809/how-many-decisions-do-we-make-each-day.
9. Søren Kierkegaard, *The Sickness Unto Death*, trans. Walter Lowrie (Princeton, 1941; Internet Archive), https://archive.org/stream/in.ernet.dli.2015.189042/2015.189042.The-Sickness-Unto-Death_djvu.txt.pdf.
10. Dr. Lynn Soots, quoted in Courtney E. Ackerman, "Flourishing in Positive Psychology: Definition + 8 Practical Tips (PDF)," PositivePsychology.com, https://positivepsychology.com/flourishing/.
11. Sheldon Vanauken, *A Severe Mercy* (New York: HarperCollins, 1980), 136.
12. Vanauken, *A Severe Mercy*, 187.
13. Jurgen Moltmann as quoted in Philip Yancey, *Where Is God When It Hurts?* Kindle Edition (Grand Rapids, MI: Zondervan, 2002), 229.
14. Richard J. Foster, *Celebration of Discipline: The Path to Spiritual Growth* (New York: HarperCollins, 1998), 108–09.

15. Vincent Ferré, *"Leaf by Niggle*: The Hidden Nucleus," The Tolkien Estate, https://www.tolkienestate.com/en/learning/specific-works/leaf-by-niggle-hidden-nucleus.html.

Chapter 3: Into the Deep

1. Rumi, *The Essential Rumi*, trans. Coleman Barks (New York: HarperCollins, 1995), 142.

2. Peter Scazzero, *Emotionally Healthy Spirituality: It's Impossible to Be Spiritually Mature, While Remaining Emotionally Immature* (Grand Rapids: Zondervan, 2017), 40.

3. Shaya Karlinsky, "Pirkei Avot: Perek 1: Chapter 1: Mishna 4," Torah.org, https://torah.org/learning/maharal-p1m4/.

4. Dietrich Bonhoeffer, *The Cost of Discipleship* (New York: Touchstone, 1959), 93.

5. Dave Eggers, *The Circle*, Kindle Edition (New York: Knopf Doubleday Publishing Group, 2013), 322.

6. SWNS, "More Than 60% of Americans Rarely Feel Rested and Energized in the Morning," *New York Post*, May 27, 2020, https://nypost.com/2020/05/27/more-than-60-percent-of-americans-rarely-feel-rested-and-energized-in-the-morning/.

7. D. A. Carson, *Scandalous: The Cross and Resurrection of Jesus* (Wheaton, IL: Crossway, 2010), 147.

8. Thomas Merton, quoted in Brennan Manning, *The Ragamuffin Gospel*, 25.

9. "Nero as the Antichrist," https://penelope.uchicago.edu/~grout/encyclopaedia_romana/gladiators/nero.html.

10. Some textual scholars question the authorship of 2 Peter, suggesting it may have been cowritten by Jude at Peter's request, or by someone anonymously. Based on my own research, however, I believe that Peter wrote it: A not-so-subtle clue is verse 1, where Peter claims to be the author! For an in-depth analysis, see Hampton Keathley IV, "The Authorship of Second Peter," Bible.org, June 3, 2004, https://bible.org/article/authorship-second-peter.

11. N. T. Wright, *After You Believe: Why Christian Character Matters* (New York: HarperOne, 2010), 32.

12. Frederick Buechner, *Wishful Thinking: A Theological ABC* (New York: Harper and Row, 1973), 118.
13. Miroslav Volf, *Free of Charge: Giving and Forgiving in a Culture Stripped of Grace*, Kindle Edition (Grand Rapids, MI: Zondervan, 2006), 44.

Chapter 4: Breathe Again

1. Mark Price, "Determined Stray Dog Tries 5 Times to Steal a Stuffed Unicorn from NC Dollar General," *News & Observer*, April 7, 2021, https://www.newsobserver.com/news/nation-world/national /article250165345.html.
2. Mark Cartwright, "The Role of Women in the Roman World," World History Encyclopedia, February 22, 2014, https://www.worldhistory .org/article/659/the-role-of-women-in-the-roman-world.
3. Mother Teresa, "On Prayer," in *The Power of Prayer*, ed. Dale Salwak (Novato, CA: New World Library, 1998), 4.
4. Thomas Pynchon, *Gravity's Rainbow* (New York: Penguin, 1973), 517.
5. Gene Weingarten, "Pearls Before Breakfast: Can One of the Nation's Great Musicians Cut Through the Fog of a D.C. Rush Hour? Let's Find Out.," *Washington Post*, April 8, 2007, https://www.washingtonpost.com /lifestyle/magazine/pearls-before-breakfast-can-one-of-the-nations-great -musicians-cut-through-the-fog-of-a-dc-rush-hour-lets-find-out/2014 /09/23/8a6d46da-4331-11e4-b47c-f5889e061e5f_story.html?itid=lk _inline_manual_4.
6. Blaise Pascal, *Pensées and Other Writings*, trans. Honor Levi, ed. Anthony Levi (Oxford: Oxford University Press, 1995), 44.
7. Kevin McSpadden, "You Now Have a Shorter Attention Span Than a Goldfish," *Time*, May 14, 2015, https://time.com/3858309/attention -spans-goldfish/.
8. Timothy Keller, *Prayer: Experiencing Awe and Intimacy with God* (New York: Penguin, 2014), 18.
9. M. K. Gandhi, *Truth Is God: Gleanings from the Writings of Mahatma Gandhi Bearing on God, God Realization and the Godly Way* (New Dehli, India: Prabhat Prakashan Publishers, 2015), 33.

10. K. Connie Kang, "Presbyterians and the Trinity: Let Us Phrase," *Los Angeles Times,* June 30, 2006.

11. John Moore, "John Moore: Unfortunately for Romney, Eastwood's Speech Was No Laughing Matter," *National Post*, August 31, 2012, https://nationalpost.com/opinion/john-moore-unfortunately-for -romney-eastwoods-speech-was-no-laughing-matter.

12. "Infanticide in the Ancient World," Early Church History, https:// earlychurchhistory.org/medicine/infanticide-in-the-ancient-world/.

13. Rev. J.C. Ryle, *A Call to Prayer* (New York: American Tract Society, 1840), 14.

Chapter 5: Live Without Walls

1. Sarah Perez, "Consumers Now Average 4.2 Hours Per Day in Apps, up 30% from 2019," TechCrunch, April 8, 2021, https://techcrunch.com/2021/04/08 /consumers-now-average-4-2-hours-per-day-in-apps-up-30-from-2019/.

2. Julia Natfulin, "Here's How Many Times We Touch Our Phones Every Day," *Insider*, July 13, 2016, https://www.businessinsider.com /dscout-research-people-touch-cell-phones-2617-times-a-day-2016-7.

3. Daniel J. Levitin, *The Organized Mind: Thinking Straight in the Age of Information Overload* (New York: Plume, 2014), 7.

4. Taneasha White, "'Zoom Fatigue' Is Real—Here's How to Cope (and Make It Through Your Next Meeting)," Healthline, February 22, 2021, https://www.healthline.com/health/zoom-fatigue#symptoms.

5. BJ Fogg, *Tiny Habits: The Small Changes That Change Everything* (Boston: Houghton Mifflin Harcourt, 2020), 4.

6. C. S. Lewis, *The Great Divorce*: *Collected Letters of C. S. Lewis*, Kindle Edition (New York: HarperOne, 2009), 43.

7. Bill Buford, "The Seductions of Story Telling," *New Yorker*, June 24, 1996, https://www.newyorker.com/magazine/1996/06/24/the-seductions -of-story-telling.

8. Nicholas Mancall-Bitel, "How to Drink, According to Frank Sinatra," Thrillist, September 14, 2016, https://www.thrillist.com/culture/frank -sinatra-quotes-on-drinking.

9. "Prayers of Augustine: St. Augustine on Prayer," Villanova University Mission & Ministry, https://www1.villanova.edu/villanova/mission/campusministry/RegularSpiritualPractices/resources/spirituality/restlesshearts/prayers.html.

10. Saint Teresa of Avila as quoted in Peter Scazzero, *Emotionally Healthy Spirituality: It's Impossible to Be Spiritually Mature, While Remaining Emotionally Immature*, Kindle Edition (Grand Rapids, MI: Zondervan, 2014), 39.

11. Parker J. Palmer, *A Hidden Wholeness: The Journey Toward an Undivided Life* (San Francisco: Jossey-Bass, 2004), 4–5.

12. Peter Scazzero and Warren Bird, *The Emotionally Healthy Church: A Strategy for Discipleship that Actually Changes Lives* (Grand Rapids: Zondervan, 2003), 147.

13. Albert Camus, *Notebooks*, 1935–1951.

14. "How an Aspiring Instagram Influencer Paid Off Her $10K Debt in 14 Months," *ABC News*, https://abcnews.go.com/GMA/Living/video/aspiring-instagram-influencer-paid-off-10k-debt-14-53727332.

15. Emily Dickinson, "I Dwell in Possibility," Poetry Foundation, https://www.poetryfoundation.org/poems/52197/i-dwell-in-possibility-466.

Chapter 6: Confronting Your Shadow Side

1. Mark Twain, *Following the Equator: A Journey Around the World* (Hartford, 1898; Project Gutenberg, 2006), https://www.gutenberg.org/files/2895/2895-h/2895-h.htm.

2. Archbishop Francois Fénelon, *Spiritual Letters of Archbishop Fénelon: Letters to Women* (London: Rivingtons, 1877), 27.

3. "Why It Is Good to Feel Regret," BBC, https://www.bbc.co.uk/programmes/articles/53rh7sYP8rRLWqSXXx6Tkkd/why-it-is-good-to-feel-regret.

4. Hermann Hesse, *Demian: The Story of Emil Sinclair's Youth*, trans. Damion Searls (New York: Penguin, 2013), 91.

5. Dietrich Bonhoeffer as quoted in Eric Metaxas, *Bonhoeffer: Pastor, Martyr, Prophet, Spy*, Kindle Edition (Nashville: Thomas Nelson, 2011), 187.

6. William Blake, *The Marriage of Heaven and Hell: A Facsimile in Full Color* (1994; repr., New York: Dover Publications, 2012), 3.

7. Robert A. Johnson, *Owning Your Own Shadow: Understanding the Dark Side of the Psyche* (New York: HarperCollins, 1991), 38.

Chapter 7: Unstoppable

1. A. W. Tozer, "January 11: Longing for God," *Tozer for the Christian Leader: A 365-Day Devotional* (Chicago: Moody, 2001).
2. Angela Duckworth, *Grit: The Power of Passion and Perseverance* (New York: Scribner, 2016), 23–24.
3. Duckworth, *Grit*, 118.
4. N. T. Wright, *After You Believe*, 20.
5. This is the title of a thought-provoking book by Eugene Peterson, *A Long Obedience in the Same Direction: Discipleship in an Instant Society* (Downers Grove, IL: InterVarsity Press Books, 2000).
6. C. S. Lewis, *The Great Divorce: Collected Letters of C. S. Lewis*, Kindle Edition (New York: HarperOne, 2009), 132.
7. Religion News Service, "The Science of Sabbath: How People Are Rediscovering Rest—and Claiming Its Benefits," *Banner*, February 17, 2019, https://www.thebanner.org/news/2019/02/the-science-of-sabbath -how-people-are-rediscovering-rest-and-claiming-its-benefits.
8. Sheryl Sandberg and Nell Scovell, *Lean In: Women, Work, and the Will to Lead* (New York: Alfred A. Knopf, 2013), 125–26.
9. Mark Buchanan, *The Holy Wild: Trusting in the Character of God* (Colorado Springs: Multnomah, 2003), 222.
10. Shoutout to my friend Drew Dyck, who has an excellent book by that name. Drew Dyck, *Your Future Self Will Thank You: Secrets to Self-Control and Brain Science* (Chicago: Moody Publishers, 2019).
11. Joshua Axelrod, "'Aggressive Arousal' and the Art of Faking It: Why the Sounds of the Game Matter to Fans and Athletes," *Toronto Star*, July 19, 2020, https://www.thestar.com/sports/soccer/analysis/2020/07/19/ aggressive-arousal-and-the-art-of-faking-it-why-the-sounds-of-the-game -matter-to-fans-and-athletes.html.
12. Ty Schalter, "How Do NFL Fans Really Affect Games?" *Bleacher Report*, December 12, 2013, https://bleacherreport.com/articles /1885183-how-does-the-12th-man-really-affect-nfl-games.

13. Patrick Rothfuss, *The Name of the Wind* (London: Gollancz, 2017), 690.

Chapter 8: Castles of the Mind

1. QMI Agency, "Missing Woman Unwittingly Joins Search Party Looking for Herself," *Toronto Sun*, August 28, 2012, https://torontosun.com/2012/08/28/missing-woman-unwittingly-joins-search-party-for-herself/.
2. Yahoo News Australia, "Why This Hilarious Missing Person Story Has Raised Eyebrows," September 15, 2019, https://au.news.yahoo.com/woman-missing-in-iceland-turns-up-as-part-of-search-party-030719609.html.
3. W. E. Vine, Merrill F. Unger, and William White Jr., *Vine's Complete Expository Dictionary of Old and New Testament Words* (Nashville: Thomas Nelson, 1996), s.v. "godliness, godly," 272.
4. Steven R. Quartz and Terrence J. Sejnowski, *Liars, Lovers, and Heroes: What the New Brain Science Reveals About How We Become Who We Are* (New York: Quill, 2002), 3.
5. Debbie Hampton, "How Your Thoughts Change Your Brain, Cells and Genes," Huffpost, March 23, 2016, https://www.huffpost.com/entry/how-your-thoughts-change-your-brain-cells-and-genes_b_9516176.
6. Elizabeth R. Thornton, "You Are Not Alone and You Are Not a Victim of Your Mind," *Psychology Today*, March 18, 2015, https://www.psychologytoday.com/us/blog/the-objective-leader/201503/you-are-not-alone-and-you-are-not-victim-your-mind.
7. Centre for Clinical Interventions, "Back from the Bluez: Module 3: The Thinking-Feeling Connection," Government of Western Australia, https://www.cci.health.wa.gov.au/-/media/CCI/Consumer-Modules/Back-from-The-Bluez/Back-from-the-Bluez---03---The-Thinking-Feeling-Connection.pdf.
8. Caroline Leaf, *Switch On Your Brain: The Key to Peak Happiness, Thinking, and Health* (Grand Rapids: Baker, 2013), 75.
9. IANS, "How Religion, Spirituality Influence Health," *Business Standard*, March 29, 2014, https://www.business-standard.com/article/news-ians/how-religion-spirituality-influence-health-114032900207_1.html.

10. Leaf, *Switch On Your Brain*, 83.

11. Earl Nightingale, "The Fog of Worry (Only 8% of Worries are Worth It)," Nightingale Conent, https://www.nightingale.com/articles/the-fog-of-worry-only-8-of-worries-are-worth-it/.

12. John Chrysostom, quoted in Joe Rutherford, "Becoming Most Useful in a Hidden, Holy Place," *Daily Journal*, August 16, 2014, https://www.djournal.com/opinion/becoming-most-useful-in-a-hidden-holy-place/article_2c341ce6-1acd-5198-9a7e-50bbcd1ffcbc.html.

13. Brittney Schrick, "Strengthen Your Brain with Gratitude," Family Life Fridays (blog), University of Arkansas Division of Agriculture, September 23, 2021, https://www.uaex.uada.edu/life-skills-wellness/personal-family-well-being/family-life-fridays-blog/posts/Gratitude.FLF.aspx.

14. Erika Stoerkel, "The Science and Research on Gratitude and Happiness," PositivePsychology.com, October 9, 2021, https://positivepsychology.com/gratitude-happiness-research/.

15. Harvard Health Publishing, "Giving Thanks Can Make You Happier," Harvard Medical School, August 14, 2021, https://www.health.harvard.edu/healthbeat/giving-thanks-can-make-you-happier.

16. Robert Emmons, "How Gratitude Can Help You Through Hard Times," *Greater Good Magazine*, May 13, 2013, https://greatergood.berkeley.edu/article/item/how_gratitude_can_help_you_through_hard_times.

Chapter 9: Closer Than a Brother

1. Susan S. Phillips, *The Cultivated Life: From Ceaseless Striving to Receiving Joy* (Downers Grove, IL: InterVarsity Press Books, 2015), 182.

2. John O'Donohue, *Anam Cara: A Book of Celtic Wisdom* (New York: Cliff Street, 1997), 13.

3. I'm indebted to Timothy Keller's 2005 sermon: "Friendship" for this insight. See Timothy J. Keller, Timothy Keller Sermon Archive (New York City: Redeemer Presbyterian Church, 2013).

4. Glenn Ruffenach, "The Pros and Cons of Moving Closer to Your Children," *Wall Street Journal*, April 10, 2017, https://www.wsj.com/articles/the-pros-and-cons-of-moving-closer-to-your-children-1491574086.

5. Henri J. M. Nouwen, *Out of Solitude* (Notre Dame, IN: Ave Maria Press, 1974), 34.

6. Stephanie Pappas, "7 Ways Friendships Are Great for Your Health," *Live Science*, January 8, 2016, https://www.livescience.com/53315 -how-friendships-are-good-for-your-health.html.

7. Erik Wilkinson, MSW, LCSW, "Build Your Own Self-Compassion Meditation," University of Kentucky, November 17, 2020, https://www .uky.edu/hr/thrive/11-17-2020/build-your-own-self-compassion -meditation.

8. Cicero, *On Old Age and Friendship*, trans. Frank Copley (Ann Arbor: University of Michigan Press, 1967), 83.

9. Corrie ten Boom, *Clippings from My Notebook* (Nashville, TN: Thomas Nelson, 1982), 19.

Chapter 10: Between Two Faces

1. Sean Giggy, "Azle Residents Find Comfort in a Stranger Who's Willing to Listen," WFAA.com, August 9, 2021, https://www.wfaa.com/article /life/heartwarming/azle-residents-find-comfort-in-a-stranger-who -listens-to-them/287-03778572-9334-4240-99a1-b7d645028b0f.

2. "Man Sets Up Tent at Azle Intersection to Simply Listen to Others," Fox4news.com, July 30, 2021, https://www.fox4news.com/news /man-sets-up-tent-at-azle-intersection-to-simply-listen-to-others.

3. Kenneth Reinhard, "The Ethics of the Neighbor: Universalism, Particularism, Exceptionalism," *Journal of Textual Reasoning*, http://jtr .shanti.virginia.edu/volume-4-number-1/the-ethics-of-the-neighbor -universalism-particularism-exceptionalism/.

4. Leo Tolstoy, *War and Peace*, trans. Louise and Aylmer Maude (Project Gutenberg, 2001), https://www.gutenberg.org/files/2600/2600-h /2600-h.htm.

5. Neel Burton, "These Are the 7 Types of Love," *Psychology Today*, June 25, 2016. https://www.psychologytoday.com/us/blog/hide-and -seek/201606/these-are-the-7-types-love.

6. Larry J. Young, "Love: Neuroscience Reveals All," *Nature* 457, no. 148 (2009), https://www.nature.com/articles/457148a.

7. Zoe Williams, "Me! Me! Me! Are We Living Through a Narcissism Epidemic?" *Guardian*, March 2, 2016, https://www.theguardian.com /lifeandstyle/2016/mar/02/narcissism-epidemic-self-obsession-attention -seeking-oversharing.

8. Monica Beyer, "Social Media Photo Overkill May Boost Narcissism," *Medical News Today*, December 3, 2018, https://www.medicalnewstoday .com/articles/323830.

9. Grant Hilary Brenner, "Why Are Narcissistic People Prone to Depression?" *Psychology Today*, February 9, 2020, https://www.psychologytoday.com/us /blog/experimentations/202002/why-are-narcissistic-people-prone -depression.

10. Amanda MacMillan, "Being Generous Really Does Make You Happier," *Time*, https://time.com/collection/guide-to-happiness/4857777/generosity -happiness-brain/.

11. "What Are the Health Benefits of Altruism?" Mental Health Foundation, https://www.mentalhealth.org.uk/publications/doing-good-does you good /health-benefits-altruism.

12. Daniel Goleman, *Social Intelligence: The New Science of Human Relationships* (New York: Bantam, 2006), 52–53.

13. Thomas à Kempis, *Of the Imitation of Christ: Four Books* (United Kingdom: H. Frowde, Oxford University Press, 1923), 84.

14. Rabbi Jonathan Sacks, *To Heal a Fractured World: The Ethics of Responsibility* (New York: Schocken, 2005), 32.

15. Sacks, 54.

16. Lindsay Baker, "Banksy: Off the Wall," *Telegraph*, March 28, 2008, https:// www.telegraph.co.uk/culture/art/3672135/Banksy-off-the-wall.html.

17. Allen Kim, "A New Banksy Mural Showed up Just in Time for Valentine's Day," CNN.com, February 14, 2020, https://www.cnn .com/style/article/banksy-new-bristol-trnd/index.html.

18. Frederich Buechner, *Secrets in the Dark: A Life in Sermons* (New York: HarperCollins, 2007), 161.

19. Saad Shaikh, MD and James Leonard-Amodeo, "The Deviating Eyes of Michelangelo's David," *Journal of the Royal Society of Medicine* 98, no. 2 (February 2005): https://www.ncbi.nlm.nih.gov/pmc/articles/PMC1079389/.

20. Adapted from N. T. Wright, who said: "I've often put it like this, if somebody you know has been very ill, you say, 'Poor old so and so, he's just a shadow of his former self.' And the extraordinary truth in the New Testament is that if you are in Christ and dwell by the spirit you are just a shadow of your *future* self." Martin Bashir, "Bishop's Heaven: Is There Life After the Afterlife?" *ABC News*, March 28, 2008, https://abcnews.go.com/Nightline/FaithMatters/story?id =4330823&page=1.
21. James K. A. Smith, *You Are What You Love: The Spiritual Power of Habit* (Grand Rapids, MI: Brazos Press, 2016), 2.

The Story You Were Made For

1. This is often attributed to Hans Urs von Balthasar; however, its true source is unknown.
2. "Authorities Say Thieves Stole House, Brick by Brick," *Midland Reporter-Telegram*, March 22, 2005, https://www.mrt.com/news /article/Authorities-say-thieves-stole-house-brick-by-7562963.php.

ABOUT THE AUTHOR

DOMINIC DONE is founder of Pursuing Faith and author of *When Faith Fails: Finding God in the Shadow of Doubt*. With a master's in theology from the University of Oxford, he has served as a pastor in Portland, Oregon; North Carolina; and Hawaii. Dominic has also been a professor at George Fox University, taught English for companies in Europe, and lived as a missionary in Vanuatu and Mexico. He and his wife, Elyssa, have a daughter, Amelia, and a fuzzy Goldendoodle, Bella.